Student Workbook

The Art of
HELPING

TENTH EDITION

Robert R. Carkhuff, Ph.D.
with
Donald M. Benoit, M.Ed.

For use with *The Art of Helping,* 10th Edition, by Robert R. Carkhuff with Donald M. Benoit

TENTH EDITION

Published by: HRD Press, Inc.
              22 Amherst Road
              Amherst, MA 01002
              800-822-2801 (U.S. and Canada)
              413-253-3488
              413-253-3490 (fax)
              http://www.hrdpress.com

ISBN 978-1-61014-426-1

Production services by Jean Miller
Cover design by Eileen Klockars

Table of Contents

List of Exercises

Post-Test

Helper Communication Scales

Pre-Test Ratings and Scoresheet

Answers

About This Workbook Edition

This workbook has been designed to match the 10th edition of *The Art of Helping* text. Learning about effective skills for helping is a valuable experience. Practicing these same skills is essential for incorporating them into your helping behaviors.

In this workbook edition, the substance of *The Art of Helping* skills remain the same. Yet, the content of nearly every exercise in this 10th edition workbook has been modified or replaced. Helpee excerpts and example helper responses have been updated and improved. Substantive explanations have been expanded and exercise directions changed or clarified. Many new exercises have been added.

We are pleased to provide you with this 10th edition of *The Art of Helping Student Workbook*.

Acknowledgements

We wish to express our grateful appreciation to Dr. Debra Decker Anderson (American International College), Mr. John Linder (Delaware County Community College), and Ms. Cheryl McLaughlin (Northern Virginia Community College) for their significant contributions to previous versions of this workbook. Although a majority of the helpee excerpts and helper responses have been modified or replaced, much of their notable workbook design has been retained.

RRC and DMB

I Introduction

# **①** Introduction

This workbook is designed to help students and practitioners make the transition from reading about the helping skills in *The Art of Helping* to practicing these skills. The workbook does not replace a skilled professor or trainer, but serves as a supplement to your coursework or training. This series of exercises will give you an opportunity to practice using the helping skills in a wide variety of written helpee situations.

In addition to the use of this workbook and *The Art of Helping* text, a complete training program may include the following:

- ➢ Role playing with other trainees to practice using the skills
- ➢ Using the skills in a supervised practice experience
- ➢ Practicing the skills using additional materials from *The Art of Helping Trainer's Guide*
- ➢ Using the skills to help yourself
- ➢ Applying the skills in real-life helping situations
- ➢ Teaching the skills to helpees in real-life helping situations

This workbook has been used by students and practitioners in many professions; they include mental health therapists, rehabilitation and school counselors, teachers, nurses, nutritionists, social workers, business managers and supervisors, personnel specialists, criminal justice workers, and others. This workbook is useful for any individual who wishes to learn to relate effectively with others.

You will find that the overall organization of the workbook parallels the skills presented in *The Art of Helping* text. Each skill presented in *The Art of Helping* has corresponding exercises in this workbook. These exercises are designed to help you *discriminate* levels of good and bad helping and *communicate* high levels of these same helping skills.

The range of problems, feelings, and types of people included in the workbook exercises represents the diversity you will likely encounter when you work with people. Practice with these varied helping situations will prepare you to handle a wide range of real-life helping situations. As you learn about the helpee phases of learning, you will also gain a clear mental image of the helping process, one that will serve to guide you when helping others.

Students and practitioners find this workbook most helpful when they read the corresponding pages in *The Art of Helping* text before they begin to complete the exercises. Preceding each series of exercises, the workbook provides you with the page numbers of the corresponding section in *The Art of Helping.*

Learning the skills of helping will be an especially exciting journey because you will meet many unique individuals along the way and learn to help them. After completing this workbook, you will be more skilled and confident in your ability to help others. This workbook is an opportunity for each of you to take critical steps in mastering the "Art of Helping."

Pre-Test

Overview

Before you complete the exercises in this workbook, find out what you currently know about the skills of helping. The following two pre-tests will give you the opportunity to evaluate both your ability to *communicate* helpfully and your ability to *discriminate* helpful responses.

Part A. Pre-Test: Communicating Helping Skills

Instructions

Imagine that you have been talking with the following helpee for about 20 minutes. The helpee is a 16-year-old girl who is having problems with her parents. She says the following:

"Honestly! They treat me like I'm 12, not 16. 'Do this. Be here. No, you can't go.' Maybe I don't always act like an adult, but I think I've earned more freedom and a chance to show I am a responsible person. It's like they're afraid to let me out of their sight for fear of what I'll do. 'We know best,' they say. I can't wait 'til I can get away."

Write down what you would say to this helpee. Write the exact words you would use if you were actually speaking to this girl.

_____

_____

_____

_____

_____

_____

_____

_____

_____

_____

(Following training, you will have the skills to rate your response to this helpee. For now, you may ask an expert—your teacher or trainer—to rate your response.)

Part B. Pre-Test: Discriminating Helping Skills

Introduction

Your training also involves learning to *discriminate* whether a response is effective of not. This pre-test will give you an idea of your current level of skill at judging the effectiveness of a response.

Instructions

Imagine that a 16-year-old girl, who is having problems with her parents, has been talking with a helper for about 20 minutes. The following is an excerpt of what she has been saying:

> *"Honestly! They treat me like I'm 12, not 16. 'Do this. Be here. No, you can't go.' Maybe I don't always act like an adult, but I think I've earned more freedom and a chance to show I am a responsible person. It's like they're afraid to let me out of their sight for fear of what I'll do. 'We know best,' they say. I can't wait 'til I can get away."*

Listed below are several alternative responses that might have been made by someone trying to help this girl. Next to each response, write a number to indicate your rating of the effectiveness of that response. Use the following scale:

1.0 = Very ineffective
2.0 = Ineffective
3.0 = Minimally effective
4.0 = Very effective
5.0 = Extremely effective

_____ a. "You feel angry because your parents don't let you take responsibility for yourself."

_____ b. "It *is* a pretty tough world out there."

_____ c. "You feel discouraged because you can't demonstrate that you're mature enough to take responsibility for yourself and you want to prove yourself. A first step might be to list all the things you could do to prove you are a responsible person. Then, choose one opportunity to show your parents that you can make good choices."

_____ d. "In other words, your parents seem to be too protective; too afraid to let you grow up."

_____ e. "You're frustrated because you can't communicate to your parents that you have grown up and you want to clearly show them that you have."

(Once you have completed the discrimination pre-test you may turn to page 177 of this workbook for answers to the discrimination pre-test. You may turn to page 178 to record your ratings and calculate your discrimination score.)

Getting Ready for Training

Overview

During your training experience, you will be playing the roles of both helper and helpee. These training experiences will be much more fluid if, when serving in the role of helpee, you have a variety of topics you can explore. These topics should be issues and concerns that are *real* to you for two reasons: 1) You will eventually have to sustain exploration of a topic with others. This will require more than superficial exploration, so you will need to identify issues that you know something about. 2) The feedback given to the helper will be more accurate and meaningful if your issues and feelings are real rather than hypothetical.

Exercise 1: Expanding Topics to Explore

Introduction

In preparation for playing the role of helpee during training, it is important to give some thought to the topics, problems, and concerns you want to explore. This exercise is designed to help you expand your list of available topics.

There are three basic resources that we, as humans, have in common:

1. **Physical:** Physical systems that enable life and provide health
2. **Emotional:** Motivations and feelings that drive and reinforce us
3. **Intellectual:** Brainpower that we use to engage with our stimulus environments

These basic resources are applied in the following areas:

➤ **Living:** Home and social settings
➤ **Learning:** School or other learning environments
➤ **Working:** Job setting

By creating a matrix with those resources and areas of functioning, you can begin to systematically expand your list of topics and explore issues within each category.

Example Matrix:

	PHYSICAL	EMOTIONAL	INTELLECTUAL
WORKING	Recent illness causes me to "call in sick" and miss work.	Not happy about current job. I dislike going to work at this job.	Having difficulty completing _____ (a specific work assignment).
LEARNING	Sometimes too tired to study in the evening after a day's activities.	I want a new, meaningful direction for what to study next.	Bad grades. Having difficulties meeting expectations in a particular course.
LIVING	Difficulty overcoming _____ (physical disability).	Feel socially unfulfilled. Would like to have a boyfriend/girlfriend to share life experiences with.	Unsure of solution for mending unhealthy/broken interpersonal relationship.

Instructions

Using the matrix on the next page, begin to expand your list of topics. Within each cell, ask yourself, "What is happening in this part of my life that I am willing to explore with others?" The topics don't have to be major problems. They may be about something positive. They *do* have to be topics that will provide others, who will be practicing their helping skills, a chance to work with you.

You can refer back to this matrix throughout the course of your training and update your list as other possible topics for exploration come to mind.

TOPICS MATRIX

	INTELLECTUAL	EMOTIONAL	PHYSICAL
WORKING	1. _____ 2. _____	1. _____ 2. _____	1. _____ 2. _____
LEARNING	1. _____ 2. _____	1. _____ 2. _____	1. _____ 2. _____
LIVING	1. _____ 2. _____	1. _____ 2. _____	1. _____ 2. _____

Exercise 2: Your Helping Model
(Prior to studying *The Art of Helping*)

Introduction

The helping process involves two participants: a helpee who is seeking assistance and a helper who provides assistance. Can you outline a process or series of behaviors that helpees engage in to solve their problems? Can you also outline or list some of the behaviors that an effective helper will perform? Can you label and describe different types of verbal responses that might be most useful for helpees to hear from you, the helper, during the helping experience?

Instructions

Before reading *The Art of Helping* text, use this space below to describe the helping process. Record an outline or list of helpee behaviors, helper behaviors, and a relationship between these helper and helpee behaviors.

(This exercise provides you with an opportunity to describe your own current understanding of a "helping model." You may find that you already identify some important, valid helpee and helper processes. This exercise is a personal marker for what you already know, *not* to be graded in any way.)

Exercise 3: Carkhuff Helping Model

Instructions

After reading the first 45 pages of *The Art of Helping* text, use the space provided below to present "The Carkhuff Helping Model." List and label the helpee's *intra*personal processes and effective helper interpersonal processes. Include arrows to show how these processes relate; how the helper's behaviors facilitate the helpee's behaviors.

(Pages 34 and 45 in *The Art of Helping* text provide the information you will need. If you are already confident you can draw The Helping Model without looking at pages 34 or 45, go ahead and make the drawing.

How did you do?

II Helping Skills

❷ Attending: Involving the Helpee

Overview

The helper enables the helpee to become involved in a helping process through attending. Attending is defined as "paying attention to another person." Attending skills include: attending physically, observing, and listening.

Exercise 4: Exploring Attending Skills

Introduction

The following exercise will help you become acquainted with your own attending skills.

Instructions

Stop! Don't move a muscle until you finish reading this!

Now, look at yourself. How are you sitting? What are you wearing? What does your facial expression look like?

Exercise

1. Describe yourself.

   _____

   _____

   _____

2. From that description, what conclusions could you draw about yourself?

   _____

   _____

3. Are you sitting in a way that helps you to learn?

   _____

   _____

4. What could you change so that you would be better able to learn?

   _____

   _____

Attending Personally

Overview

Attending includes preparing the helpee, preparing the helping context, preparing ourselves, and attending personally.

Exercise 5: Discriminating Involving

Introduction

Helping will not occur unless the helpee becomes involved in the helping process. Therefore, prior to meeting with a helpee, you should inform the individual about the "who, what, when, where, why, and how (5WH)" of the proposed helping process. This is the first step in involving the person in the helping process.

The following example is a good illustration of involving because it tells *who* the appointment is with, *what* the purpose of the interview is, *when* and *where* it will be, *how* the person will get to meet Mr. Kennerly, and *why* the person should come to the interview (5WH).

> *"...your appointment is with me, Mr. Kennerly, at 10 a.m. tomorrow (**when**). My office is Room 306 here at the clinic where you came on Friday (**where**). If you come to the receptionist in the main lobby, she will text me and I will come down to meet you (**how**). During this first meeting we'll be exploring the problems you expressed at intake (**what**). Our goal will be to list and specify a starting point (**what**) so we can help you act to clear up these problems (**why**). You sound eager to start solving these problems."*

Instructions

After reading the following example, identify the 5WH in the involving exercises. Note that some important information may be missing.

Example:

Email Sent: *"Hi Carly! I'd love to meet with you to see how you're doing! How about lunch on Saturday? I'll meet you at Nick's Café at 12:30. The two of us can have a relaxing lunch and talk about the progress you've made since we last saw one another."* — Eylanna

Who: *the two of us (Carly and Elyanna)*

What: *meet for lunch*

When: *Saturday, 12:30*

Where: *Nick's Café*

Why: *to talk about the progress Carly has made*

How: *no specific directions given about how to get to the location*

Exercise

Text message sent: *"Why don't you come by the house on Monday, Sue? We can talk then."*

Who: _____

What: _____

When: _____

Where: _____

Why: _____

How: _____

Exercise 6: Practicing Involving

Introduction

This exercise will give you a chance to practice involving others.

Instructions

After reading the sample statement presented below, write a statement that you might use to involve someone in your present or planned helping specialty (i.e., social work, medicine, criminal justice, education, nursing, etc.). Be sure to include and label the 5WH information as shown in this example.

Example:

*"Hello Jennifer, this is Mark Sampson from the Career Counseling Office (**who**). I'm calling to confirm our appointment for Friday morning at 10:30 (**when**). My office is in the Bradley Building, Room 106 (**where**). If you park in the back of the building and enter by the rear entrance (**how**), my office is the first door on the right (**where**). We'll use this first session to explore what you want to learn from our career counseling sessions (**what/why**)."*

Exercise

Your involving statement:

_____

_____

_____

_____

_____

_____

_____

_____

_____

_____

Exercise 7: Discriminating Contextual Attending

Introduction

In any helping interaction, the furniture and environment should not create barriers or be distractions to the helping process.

Instructions

In this exercise, identify three environments where you often talk with friends and family. Briefly describe these contextual settings and identify their contextual strengths and deficits. An example is presented below.

Example:

Environment:	*Kitchen*
Description:	*Small kitchen with round table in front of a window.*
Contextual Strengths:	*Warm, cheerful room*
	Chairs can be moved closer or further away, as appropriate
Contextual Deficits:	*Centerpiece; miscellaneous supplies on table create a barrier*
	Family members use of kitchen can be distracting

Exercise

1. **Environment:** _____

   Description: _____

   _____

   Contextual Strengths: _____

   _____

   _____

   Contextual Deficits: _____

   _____

   _____

   _____

2. **Environment:** _____

   Description: _____

   _____

   Contextual Strengths: _____

   _____

   _____

   Contextual Deficits: _____

   _____

   _____

   _____

3. **Environment:** _____

   Description: _____

   _____

   Contextual Strengths: _____

   _____

   _____

   Contextual Deficits: _____

   _____

   _____

   _____

Exercise 8: Discriminating Self-Preparation Skills

Introduction

Prior to meeting with a helpee, you should: review what you know about him or her, identify your goal for the upcoming interaction, and eliminate or minimize any personal tension or internal distractions that you are experiencing.

Instructions

Identify the review, goal, and relaxation efforts in each of the following self-preparation stories. Read the two examples before completing the exercise.

Example 1:

Carol was having a long and very difficult day. She had two people who called for emergency appointments. She was down to the last appointment of her day, one of the emergency appointments. With a deep breath, she looked at her watch and then took a couple of minutes to read through the client's file. In particular, she read about their last session. She also tried to remember what the person had said on the phone and how the person had sounded. In her mind, she determined that she would help the person work through the emergency and then try to relate it to the goals they had already set for their time together. Finally, she sat back in her chair and closed her eyes. She took several long, deep breaths. Consciously, she relaxed the muscles of her face, neck, shoulders, and the rest of her body. Once she was finished, she got up and went to the door to greet the waiting person.

Prepare Yourself

Review information about the helpee: *Read through the helpee's file.*

Review meeting goal(s):   *Work through emergency. Relate emergency to previously agreed-upon goals.*

Relax (eliminate internal distractions):   *Deep breathing, relax muscles. Accept the fact that this has been a busy day.*

Example 2:

Chris was late getting into the office. He had overslept, exhausted from an active and fun weekend. His first appointment, Evelyn, was waiting. Glancing at his watch, he knew he was going to be behind schedule for the rest of the day.

Chris entered the waiting room to find Evelyn already there. "Good morning, Evelyn. How are you today?"

"I'm fine, Chris."

"Sorry to keep you waiting. Let me get a cup of coffee and we'll get started."

Chris got himself a cup of coffee, took it into the office, and then looked at his desk. There was a note informing him that one client had cancelled his appointment for later than morning. He smiled. It meant that he would catch up and even have a breathing space during the day. Still smiling, he went to the door and invited Evelyn into his office.

Prepare Yourself

Review information about the helpee: *None—did not do it*

Review meeting goal(s): *None—did not do it*

Relax (eliminate internal distractions): *Cup of coffee (not relaxing). Still distracted (smiling about how fortunate he was to have an upcoming cancellation).*

Exercise

1. Joyce was regretting her upcoming appointment in her home office. Joyce did not want to see Katherine, not today and not in her home. On top of that, everything that could go wrong had gone wrong that day. The weather was hot and humid. The bus broke down on the way home so she had to walk the last quarter mile. Her air conditioner was broken and she didn't have time for a shower before Katherine would arrive. All she could think of was how hot, tired, and hungry she was and how badly she did not want to see Katherine. As Joyce was thinking this very thought, the doorbell rang.

   She opened the door to let Katherine in, greeting her with a distracted, tired, "Hi, come on in."

Prepare Yourself

Review information about the helpee:

_____

_____

_____

_____

Review meeting goal(s):

_____

_____

_____

_____

Relax (eliminate internal distractions):

_____

_____

_____

_____

Exercise (continued)

2. Marsha Miller walked down the hall to her office. Standing outside her door was one of her students, Mark. Mark was going to get a failing grade unless something drastic happened. As she got to the door, Mark said, "Hi, Dr. Miller. Could I talk with you about class?"

   "Sure, Mark. Just give me a few minutes. Wait here, okay?"

   Marsha went into her office and settled behind her desk. She took out her class records of Mark's class and reviewed his test scores and attendance. She noticed that he had done well on his two assigned papers, but not good enough to pass. With a sigh, she sat back and closed her eyes, letting her mind clear naturally. After a couple of minutes, she went to the door and said, "Come on in, Mark."

Prepare Yourself

Review information about the helpee:

_____

_____

_____

_____

Review meeting goal(s):

_____

_____

_____

_____

Relax (eliminate internal distractions):

_____

_____

_____

_____

(Exercise 8 answers are on page 179.)

Exercise 9: Practicing Self-Preparation

Introduction

This exercise will give you a chance to see how self-preparation applies to you and your relationships.

Instructions

Select someone that you know and like. Then...

1. Write a brief description of your past two interactions with this person.

2. Write a goal for your next interaction.

3. Describe a way that you can relax and eliminate internal distractions before the actual interaction.

Exercise 10: Discriminating Postural Attending

Introduction

The helper's body should be positioned to communicate attention: squared, leaning forward, maintaining eye contact, and creating no distractions. A helper should also maintain an appropriate distance from the helpee.

Instructions

Observe the following people for three minutes while they are having a conversation with someone. List their postural attending deficits and assets in the space provided.

Example:

Individual being observed: A father, talking with his son in the living room about possible colleges to attend.

Postural Attending Deficits

(Leaning back in chair)

(Feet propped on coffee table)

(Not squared)

(Smoking)

Postural Attending Assets

(Good eye contact)

(Appropriate distance between father and son)

Exercise

1. **Individual being observed:** A family member, roommate, or friend

   Postural Attending Deficits

   _____

   _____

   _____

   _____

   _____

   _____

   Postural Attending Assets

   _____

   _____

   _____

   _____

   _____

   _____

Exercise (continued)

2. **Individual being observed:** A person in a store making a sale or providing information

   Postural Attending Deficits

   _____

   _____

   _____

   _____

   _____

   _____

   _____

   Postural Attending Assets

   _____

   _____

   _____

   _____

   _____

   _____

   _____

3. **Individual being observed:** An individual that you know talking with another person at school or work

   Postural Attending Deficits

   _____

   _____

   _____

   _____

   _____

   _____

   _____

   Postural Attending Assets

   _____

   _____

   _____

   _____

   _____

   _____

   _____

Observing

Overview

Personal attending prepares us to observe. Observing is one of the greatest sources of learning about a helpee. The following exercises will help you practice your observation skills. (See pages 84–94 in *The Art of Helping* for a detailed explanation of Observing.)

Exercise 11: Discriminating Data from Inferences

Introduction

It is important to look at concrete data first and then draw your conclusions from the data. Data consists of appearance and behaviors, for example: "a smile," "tears," or "clenched fists." In contrast, inferences are conclusions that we come to after we have seen the data. Examples include: "friendly person," "broken-hearted," and "steaming mad."

Instructions

Identify whether the following statements present data or inferences by checking the appropriate box.

Example:

	DATA	INFERENCE
Open-minded		☑
Facial tick (spasmatic muscle contraction)	☑	

Exercise

	DATA	INFERENCE
1. Seems nervous	❏	❏
2. Ready to relate	❏	❏
3. Chewing lower lip, frowning, tapping foot	❏	❏
4. Looks excited	❏	❏
5. 5'8", broad shoulders, well-defined muscles	❏	❏
6. Overweight by 20 pounds, shirttail hanging out, patched jeans	❏	❏
7. Attractive person	❏	❏
8. Looks like a con man—untrustworthy, sly	❏	❏
9. Eyes squint, looks away, slouches	❏	❏
10. Seems to be thinking about getting away	❏	❏
11. Guilty face if I ever saw one	❏	❏
12. Pale yellow skin, fast breath, hard pulse in neck	❏	❏
13. Slumping down in chair, round shoulders, leaning back, legs straight out	❏	❏
14. Approximately 40 years old, wearing modern suit, tie matched for color, carrying briefcase, shoulders upright	❏	❏
15. Looks sad and obviously distressed about her life, a very unhappy person	❏	❏
16. Wealthy person	❏	❏
17. High energy level	❏	❏
18. Doesn't care about what others think of him	❏	❏
19. Sitting upright, fully squared, direct eye contact, no nervous habits	❏	❏
20. Looks whacky as a fruitcake; a classic	❏	❏

(Exercise 11 answers are on page 179.)

Exercise 12: Drawing Inferences from Observations

Introduction

How our helpees look and act tell us a great deal about what their energy levels are and how they are feeling. Often, we can make inferences about their levels of physical and emotional readiness to participate in a helping session.

Instructions

Match these observations of appearance and behavior to the energy levels, feelings, and inferences for readiness that these observations might suggest. Place the letter(s) of the appropriate inferences next to the observations.

Example:

	OBSERVATIONS	INFERENCES
a, c, e	Gesturing wildly, smiling	a. High energy
b, d, f	Eyes half open	b. Low energy
		c. Good, happy, positive feelings
		d. Sad, weak feelings
		e. High intellectual readiness
		f. Low intellectual readiness

Exercise

	OBSERVATIONS	INFERENCES
1.	_____ Concentrating on tasks	a. High energy
2.	_____ Head resting on arm, legs outstretched	b. Low energy
3.	_____ Clean hair and clothes, fashionable, coordinated clothing	c. Good, happy, positive feelings
		d. Sad, weak feelings
4.	_____ Facing away from group	e. High intellectual readiness
5.	_____ Laughing and smiling	f. Low intellectual readiness
6.	_____ Facing members of the group and making eye contact when they speak	
7.	_____ Yawning	
8.	_____ Extremely thin woman—5'6", 105 lbs.	
9.	_____ Slouched posture	
10.	_____ Dark circles underneath bloodshot eyes	

(Exercise 12 answers are on page 179.)

Exercise 13: Observing Effectively

Introduction

You have now had some practice discriminating data from inferences. The next exercise will help you organize and draw appropriate inferences. When practicing observing skills, it can be helpful to organize your observations and inferences on a chart like those on the pages that follow. The charts will help you to check your observations of appearance and behavior for completeness and accuracy.

Instructions

Complete three observations of people using the following steps:

1. Select people for observation as designated on the following pages.

2. Observe each person for at least three minutes.

3. Using the charts on the next few pages, record your observations of appearance and behavior.

4. Based on these observations, circle your inferences about each person's energy level.

5. Circle your inferences about each person's feelings.

Example:

Situation: Observation of a young man standing on a street corner.

Appearance	Behavior	Inference
Posture: Standing slouched, leaning against a building **Facial Expressions:** Loosely hanging mouth, eyes downcast **Grooming:** Torn t-shirt, dirty jeans, dirty sneakers with holes, shaggy haircut, hair hanging in eyes **Body Build:** About 6 feet tall and 150 pounds, thin **Sex:** Male **Age:** Early 20's **Race:** White	**Body Movements:** Slow hand and arm movements while smoking a cigarette	**Energy Level:** High — Medium — (Low) **Feelings:** Up — Mixed — (Down)

Exercise

1. **Situation:** Observe a person you know well, in school or at work.

Appearance	Behavior	Inference
Posture: **Facial Expressions:** **Grooming:** **Body Build:** **Sex:** **Age:** **Race:**	**Body Movements:**	**Energy Level:** High — Medium — Low **Feelings:** Up — Mixed — Down

2. **Situation:** Observe a person you know slightly, in school or at work.

Appearance	Behavior	Inference
Posture: **Facial Expressions:** **Grooming:** **Body Build:** **Sex:** **Age:** **Race:**	**Body Movements:**	**Energy Level:** High — Medium — Low **Feelings:** Up — Mixed — Down

Exercise (continued)

3. **Situation:** Observe a person you do not know.

Appearance	Behavior	Inference
Posture: **Facial Expressions:** **Grooming:** **Body Build:** **Sex:** **Age:** **Race:**	**Body Movements:**	**Energy Level:** High — Medium — Low **Feelings:** Up — Mixed — Down

Exercise 14: Practicing Attending Skills

Introduction

This exercise will help you apply all of your attending skills in a familiar context.

Instructions

Watch a TV program. Attend physically while watching the program. After 10 minutes, complete the following exercise.

Exercise

1. Check your own physical attending.

   - **Attending contextually:** Was the room arranged so that you had an excellent view of the TV set? Was the room arranged for your comfort?

     ❏ Yes   ❏ No

     If no to either question, what was wrong? _____

     _____

     _____

   - **Attending personally:** Were you hungry or tired while watching?

     ❏ Yes   ❏ No

     If yes, what was wrong? _____

     _____

     _____

2. Name or otherwise identify two characters that you found to be interesting.

   Character #1: _____

   Character #2: _____

   For each character, after observing and listening, complete the following observation chart and answer the questions provided.

Exercise (continued)

Character #1

- Observing the character:

Appearance	Behavior	Inference
Posture: Facial Expressions: Grooming: Body Build: Sex: Age: Race:	Body Movements:	Energy Level: High — Medium — Low Feelings: Up — Mixed — Down

- Listening to the character:

With whom did the character speak? _____

_____

What did they talk about? _____

_____

_____

When did this occur? _____

Where did this occur? _____

Why did they speak with each other? _____

_____

How (process) or how well (quality) did the conversation go? _____

_____

_____

Exercise (continued)

Character #2

- Observing the character:

Appearance	Behavior	Inference
Posture:	Body Movements:	Energy Level:
		High — Medium — Low
Facial Expressions:		
		Feelings:
Grooming:		Up — Mixed — Down
Body Build:		
Sex:		
Age:		
Race:		

- Listening to the character:

With whom did the character speak? _____

_____

What did they talk about? _____

_____

_____

When did this occur? _____

Where did this occur? _____

Why did they speak with each other? _____

_____

How (process) or how well (quality) did the conversation go? _____

_____

_____

❸ Responding: Facilitating Helpee Exploring

Overview

In this section, you will learn to *respond* or verbally communicate your understanding of the helpee's experiences. You will communicate your understanding by responding at an interchangeable level to the content, feelings, and meaning expressed by the helpee.

The exercises contained in this section will first teach you "Responding to Content." Next, you will learn "Responding to Feeling." Finally, you will combine them in "Responding to Meaning." Refer to pages 111–145 in *The Art of Helping* text for information about responding.

Exercise 15: Exploring Responding Skills

Introduction

This exercise will help you become acquainted with the importance of responding. When you respond, you communicate an openness to another person's point of view.

Instructions

Take a moment to think about the importance of responding to another person's experience.

Exercise

Think of the last time you had an argument with a friend (or your mother/father/employer). Think about that argument. What did you do or say? What did the other person do or say? Would you have been more willing to explore both positions if the other person had communicated an understanding of your point of view? Why?

_____

_____

_____

_____

_____

_____

_____

_____

Responding to Content

Overview

A good response to content should paraphrase what was said as concisely as possible and without parroting all the details. To make sure you understand the skill, review pages 116–117 in *The Art of Helping*.

Exercise 16: Discriminating Specific Responses

Introduction

Responses to content should be specific, not vague. Vague responses do not facilitate exploration. Specific responses help clarify the helpee's experience which facilitates further exploration.

Instructions

Identify whether the following responses are specific or vague.

Example:

Student: *"I'm so tired, I don't know what to do. I try to keep up with everything: work, home, classes. But each day seems so long. By noon, I'm already too tired to cope."*

    a. You're saying you're tired.

        ☐ Specific   ☑ Vague

    b. You're saying there's so much to do that you don't have the energy to do it all.

        ☑ Specific   ☐ Vague

Exercise

Mother: *"My children are starting to get out of hand. They've gotten so they don't listen to me or my husband unless we threaten them. Who wants to always have to threaten their kids?"*

1. You're saying your kids are too wild.

   ☐ Specific   ☐ Vague

2. You're saying your children don't behave unless you or your husband threaten them.

   ☐ Specific   ☐ Vague

3. You're saying you don't want to have to threaten your kids to get them to follow your directions.

   ☐ Specific   ☐ Vague

4. In other words, your children don't obey until you threaten them in some way.

   ☐ Specific   ☐ Vague

5. In other words, you don't want to have to do this.

   ☐ Specific   ☐ Vague

6. You're saying you don't like this behavior.

   ☐ Specific   ☐ Vague

(Exercise 16 answers are on page 180.)

Exercise 17: Discriminating Paraphrasing vs. Parroting

Introduction

Responses to content should paraphrase the original expression and not "parrot." By using different words to express the same content, paraphrasing adds a fresh perspective and facilitates exploration.

Instructions

Identify whether the following responses "parrot" or paraphrase the original expression.

Example:

Boyfriend: *"Well, she's finally talking to me again. It's not the same, but at least we're talking. I still feel awful about the things she thinks I said about her. I would never say or do anything to hurt her. I think too much of her."*

a. You're saying she's finally talking to you even though it's not the same. You feel awful about what she thinks you said because you would never do anything to hurt her.

☑ Parrot   ☐ Paraphrase

b. You're saying that you are slowly straightening out the misunderstanding and you're talking to one another again.

☐ Parrot   ☑ Paraphrase

Exercise

1. *"I'm stuck. My boss refused to let me complete the new project my way. I didn't check with him until I'd done 40 hours of work and now I've got to redo the whole thing by Monday morning."*

   a. You're saying that you're stuck because your boss refused to let you do the project your way and now you've got to redo the whole thing by Monday morning.

   ☐ Parrot   ☐ Paraphrase

   b. You're saying that you have to invest all that effort again.

   ☐ Parrot   ☐ Paraphrase

   c. You're saying that you didn't check in time and now you're in a tight spot.

   ☐ Parrot   ☐ Paraphrase

Exercise (continued)

2. *"Thanks for all the help you've given me this semester. I was pretty mixed up when I got here, but now I really feel I've got it together. I'm passing all my courses for the first time."*

   a. You're saying that you're succeeding academically and I made a difference.

      ☐ Parrot   ☐ Paraphrase

   b. You're saying that you appreciate my help this semester. You've gotten it together and you are passing all your courses.

      ☐ Parrot   ☐ Paraphrase

   c. You're saying you feel pleased with the affect my assistance has made on your schoolwork.

      ☐ Parrot   ☐ Paraphrase

(Exercise 17 answers are on page 180.)

Exercise 18: Discriminating Brief Responses

Introduction

Responses to content should be brief without losing specificity.

Instructions

Identify whether the following responses are *too long* or *brief and specific*.

Example:

Employee: *"Damn, I blew it again! I just don't seem to be able to think before I open my big mouth. This job was going so smoothly until I got mad and told off my supervisor."*

    a. You're saying you messed up by exploding at your supervisor.

        ☐ Too Long   ☑ Brief and Specific

    b. You're saying that everything was going well but you went and messed it up by mouthing off just like you always do. Now, since you yelled at the supervisor, it isn't so good at work.

        ☑ Too Long   ☐ Brief and Specific

Exercise

Alcoholic: *"I just can't give up my drinking. I've tried and tried and I can't. I get some money in my pocket and I have good intentions, but I just buy more beer and wine."*

1. You're saying you can't quit drinking even though you've tried. You always spend your money on booze.

   ☐ Too Long ☐ Brief and Specific

2. In other words, you always buy booze even when you're trying to quit.

   ☐ Too Long ☐ Brief and Specific

3. You're saying you can't give up the beer and wine. Even though you try not to buy any, it seems like if you get money, you go to the store and that's what you spend your money on. Even having good intentions doesn't make a difference with you.

   ☐ Too Long ☐ Brief and Specific

4. In other words, you can't quit drinking. You try and try and yet it just seems that when you get money that's how you spend it. Even when you have good intentions and you're trying to quit, you buy booze with your money.

   ☐ Too Long ☐ Brief and Specific

5. You're saying giving up drinking isn't easy for you no matter how good your intentions.

   ☐ Too Long ☐ Brief and Specific

(Exercise 18 answers are on page 180.)

Exercise 19: Discriminating Good Content Responses

Introduction

This exercise will help you identify effective and ineffective responses to the content of what a helpee is saying so that you can evaluate and improve your own future responses.

Instructions

Rate each response to content and state the reason for your rating.

Example:

Student: *"I don't know…school just isn't living up to my expectations. I thought that when I got here that life would be different—that classes would be exciting, that there would be a lot of parties to go to, that I'd be doing lots of great things. But it seems that my classes just review what I already know. My buddies and I just end up sitting around and doing nothing more. School is no better than staying home and working for my father."*

1. It's too bad you feel that way. There really is a lot to do—if you go out and find it.

   Reason: *Does not indicate the helper really heard the speaker;*   **Good** ☐   **Poor** ☑

   it contradicts the helpee's statement; judgmental

2. You're saying that this is no better than home, that you expected new school work and lots of parties, but you just end up sitting around with your buddies and not doing much of anything.

   Reason: *Parrots back most of the details without*   **Good** ☐   **Poor** ☑

   summarizing the essential point; it is not brief enough

3. You're saying that school hasn't given you what you were looking for—something new and exciting.

   Reason: *Sums up what the speaker said in brief,*   **Good** ☑   **Poor** ☐

   paraphrased response

Exercise

Ball Player: *"That coach! He spent all week telling me 'This game I'll play ya,' and then at last night's game, he ignored me. No playing time!"*

1. You're saying, "That coach! He spends all week telling you 'this game I'll play ya,' and then at last night's game he ignored you." You didn't play once.

   Reason: _____ Good ☐ Poor ☐

   _____

   _____

2. You're saying the coach was rotten.

   Reason: _____ Good ☐ Poor ☐

   _____

   _____

3. You're saying the coach set you up so you expected to play and then he didn't follow through on his word.

   Reason: _____ Good ☐ Poor ☐

   _____

   _____

4. You're saying the coach wasn't too cool. He told you, "You'll play," and you were ready for it to happen. Yet, when last night's game came along, it turned out that he had really misled you. I mean, here he'd told you that you would play and then he left you sitting on the bench the whole game. You never got any playing time from that coach.

   Reason: _____ Good ☐ Poor ☐

   _____

   _____

5. In other words, the coach let you down after encouraging you and building up your expectations.

   Reason: _____ Good ☐ Poor ☐

   _____

   _____

(Exercise 19 answers are on page 180.)

Exercise 20: Practicing Good Content Responses

Introduction

Now that you had some practice in discriminating helpful responses to content, you are ready to begin developing your own responses. Writing responses will make it easier for you to make verbal responses later.

Instructions

Review the elements of a good response to content, then write your best response to the content expressed in each of the following statements.

Example:

Teenager: *"My parents are constantly checking my online school gradebook. They insist that I tell them where I am at all times. They won't let me drive the family car after 10 p.m., ever!"*

You're saying *that your parents are limiting your freedom.*

Exercise

1. **Middle-Aged Man:** *"I've been to my family doctor, specialists, and the emergency room. I've had my head checked out. I've been scoped, top-down, and bottom-up. The endocrinologist said all my bloodwork is within acceptable ranges. I still feel sick! Two years is a long time to feel ill."*

   You're saying _____

   _____

2. **Teenager:** *"I didn't do anything. I was just standing here, and some guy went running by me. I began walking in the same direction and then I heard you yell at me to stop. So I stopped."*

   You're saying _____

   _____

Exercise (continued)

3. **Teenager:** *"My friend and I were hired to repaint an apartment. We worked hard and did a great job. We trusted that the owner would pay us decently, but when we were paid, we made less than minimum wage for the hours we worked. I know that my friend and I are both still in high school, but the amount we were paid was not right."*

You're saying _____

_____

_____

4. **Employee:** *"This guy is impossible to work with. He stands over my shoulder and constantly talks. He tells me what I'm doing right, what I'm doing wrong, what to accept, what to reject, and the "right way" to do everything!"*

You're saying _____

_____

_____

5. **Student:** *"The teacher is always on my friend's back; nothing Tommy ever does is right. Every time Tommy moves, 'wrong move!' and she starts to yell at him."*

You're saying _____

_____

_____

6. **Business Woman:** *"My career just doesn't seem to be going anywhere. The choices I've made in the past have all been dead ends. There are never any future opportunities in the jobs I accept."*

You're saying _____

_____

_____

7. **Homemaker:** *"I've finally found a group of people who really offer what I want in friendships. They are mature, reliable, fun-loving, decent, and have a strong sense of who they are. They make me feel good."*

You're saying _____

_____

_____

Exercise (continued)

8. **Ex-convict:** *"I've been looking hard for work, but they don't give you a fair break once they know you've got that prison record. They judge the record, not the man. They leave no room for people who have changed."*

You're saying _____

_____

_____

9. **Patient:** *"No one has told me a thing about why I'm here in this mental hospital. I feel like I'm part of the furniture here—not a person! No one treats me like they even see me."*

You're saying _____

_____

_____

10. **Father:** *"I need help. I got laid off two months ago and we didn't have much savings. These past two months ate up our money. I can't even buy my kids new school supplies this year."*

You're saying _____

_____

_____

Responding to Feeling

Overview

When formulating a verbal response to the feelings of another person, it is useful to have a large vocabulary of feeling words available to you. From this feeling word vocabulary, you will select words that are *appropriate to the other person's frame of reference* including the selection of feeling words that are accurate in *feeling category* and accurate in *intensity*.

Before completing the exercises in this section, review pages 120–132 in *The Art of Helping.*

Exercise 21: Discriminating Accurate Feeling Responses

Introduction

Knowing if a feeling word is accurate or inaccurate prepares you to make better responses to feelings.

Some reasons that a response to feeling may not be accurate are:

➢ The category is wrong

➢ The intensity is off

➢ The response comes from the helper's frame of reference, not the frame of reference of the other person

➢ The response does not use a feeling word

Instructions

In this exercise, rate the accuracy of the feeling word in each response. After rating each response, state your reason for your rating. Use the following ratings:

(+) If the response is accurate

(–) If the response is *not* accurate

Example:

Roommate: *"I just don't understand it! I walked into my room this afternoon and my roommate totally ignored me! I asked her what was wrong; she looked at me and said, 'You should know,' then left. What am I supposed to do? She doesn't let me in on what's bothering her."*

1. **Response:** You feel that she's keeping something from you.

   Rating: ☐ (+) Accurate ☑ (−) Not accurate

   Reason: *No feeling word*

2. **Response:** You feel confused.

   Rating: ☑ (+) Accurate ☐ (−) Not accurate

   Reason: *Accurate category and intensity*

3. **Response:** You feel petrified.

   Rating: ☐ (+) Accurate ☑ (−) Not accurate

   Reason: *Inaccurate category and intensity*

Exercise

1. **Wife:** *"I don't know what's wrong between my husband and me. When we got married we were so close and now there is a void between us. We just don't communicate anymore."*

   a. **Response:** You feel disconnected.

      Rating: ☐ (+) Accurate ☐ (−) Not accurate

      Reason:

   b. **Response:** You feel enraged!

      Rating: ☐ (+) Accurate ☐ (−) Not accurate

      Reason:

   c. **Response:** You feel rejected.

      Rating: ☐ (+) Accurate ☐ (−) Not accurate

      Reason:

Exercise (continued)

2. **Dropout:** *"I missed the appointment. The damn bus was late and then it was farther to walk from the bus stop than I thought. Now I have to wait another two months to take the GED. I really wanted to get that degree now."*

    a. **Response:** You feel furious. _____

       Rating: ☐ (+) Accurate   ☐ (−) Not accurate

       Reason: _____

    b. **Response:** You feel hopeless. _____

       Rating: ☐ (+) Accurate   ☐ (−) Not accurate

       Reason: _____

    c. **Response:** You feel disappointed. _____

       Rating: ☐ (+) Accurate   ☐ (−) Not accurate

       Reason: _____

3. **Teacher:** *"The teacher's aide I have this year is immature. She acts like she's 14—and that's being kind. I don't know how I'm gonna make it through the year with her."*

    a. **Response:** You feel discouraged. _____

       Rating: ☐ (+) Accurate   ☐ (−) Not accurate

       Reason: _____

    b. **Response:** You feel irritated. _____

       Rating: ☐ (+) Accurate   ☐ (−) Not accurate

       Reason: _____

    c. **Response:** You feel devastated. _____

       Rating: ☐ (+) Accurate   ☐ (−) Not accurate

       Reason: _____

(Exercise 21 answers are on page 180.)

Exercise 22: Choosing Accurate Feeling Words

Introduction

You will often find that several different feeling words accurately capture a person's experience. You will be more likely to identify the most accurate feeling if you first explore their many possible feelings.

Instructions

Circle the feeling words that accurately identify (category and intensity) the feelings of the speaker.

Example:

Young Man: *"I finally found some people I can really get along with. There's no pretentiousness about them at all. They're real and they understand me. I can be myself with them."*

How would I feel if I were this person?

(a.) happy	d. confused	g. skeptical
b. worried	e. let down	(h.) excited
(c.) delighted	(f.) good	i. baffled

Exercise

1. **Teenage Employee:** *"I'm sick and tired of being the 'go-for' in that office. I've been working there for six months now, and I think that I should have earned some responsibility."*

    How would I feel if I were this person?

a. fed up	d. furious	g. surprised
b. happy	e. paralyzed	h. confused
c. ignored	f. amused	i. used

2. **Sibling:** *"I wish I knew what I could do. My sister and my parents are fighting again. NOTHING my sister ever does is right in their eyes—like she's damned if she does and damned if she doesn't. Yet they do have a point. Sometimes she doesn't show any sense."*

    How would I feel if I were this person?

a. intrigued	d. frustrated	g. lucky
b. troubled	e. sad	h. torn
c. excited	f. tired	i. upset

Exercise (continued)

3. **College Student:** *"I finally got up enough nerve to talk to 'Hurricane Hilda' about my paper. I was honest about the trouble I've been having. I did what we worked out; I responded to her. And it worked! I'm all set with my paper and I discovered she's human too."*

   How would I feel if I were this person?

a.	pleased	d.	insulted	g.	embarrassed
b.	let down	e.	good	h.	surprised
c.	tolerated	f.	relieved	i.	angry

4. **Drug Addict:** *"I guess when I was a teenager I felt so down all the time and 'uppers' made me feel better. I still like them, but I feel like the drug is in control, not me. I'm always hyper."*

   How would I feel if I were this person?

a.	uneasy	d.	good	g.	trapped
b.	excited	e.	scared	h.	potent
c.	confused	f.	turned on	i.	vulnerable

5. **Patient:** *"I got back the lab tests today—it's not cancer! I feel like life is beginning all over again! Fantastic!"*

   How would I feel if I were this person?

a.	relieved	d.	cautious	g.	free
b.	disappointed	e.	thrilled	h.	depressed
c.	alive	f.	foggy	i.	impatient

(Exercise 22 answers are on page 181.)

Exercise 23: Increasing Your Feeling Word Vocabulary

Introduction

This exercise is designed to help you generate a large number of feeling words. It can be used as a "think step" when you are stuck for a word to use when responding to a person.

Instructions

Take each of the stimulus words given and complete the sentence with another feeling word. Now, use the new word as your next stimulus and repeat the process. (An extensive list of feeling words can be found in Appendix A of *The Art of Helping* text.)

Example:

When I feel angry, I feel *furious.*

When I feel *furious,* I feel *burned.*

When I feel *burned,* I feel *cheated.*

When I feel *cheated,* I feel *hurt.*

When I feel *hurt,* I feel *sad.*

Exercise

1. When I feel *excited,* I feel _____.

   When I feel _____, I feel _____.

   When I feel _____, I feel _____.

   When I feel _____, I feel _____.

   When I feel _____, I feel _____.

Exercise (continued)

2. When I feel ***hopeless,*** I feel _____.

    When I feel _____, I feel _____.

    When I feel _____, I feel _____.

    When I feel _____, I feel _____.

    When I feel _____, I feel _____.

3. When I feel ***afraid,*** I feel _____.

    When I feel _____, I feel _____.

    When I feel _____, I feel _____.

    When I feel _____, I feel _____.

    When I feel _____, I feel _____.

4. When I feel ***mixed up,*** I feel _____.

    When I feel _____, I feel _____.

    When I feel _____, I feel _____.

    When I feel _____, I feel _____.

    When I feel _____, I feel _____.

5. When I feel ***sorry,*** I feel _____.

    When I feel _____, I feel _____.

    When I feel _____, I feel _____.

    When I feel _____, I feel _____.

    When I feel _____, I feel _____.

Exercise (continued)

6. When I feel *upset,* I feel _____.

    When I feel _____, I feel _____.

    When I feel _____, I feel _____.

    When I feel _____, I feel _____.

    When I feel _____, I feel _____.

7. When I feel *confident,* I feel _____.

    When I feel _____, I feel _____.

    When I feel _____, I feel _____.

    When I feel _____, I feel _____.

    When I feel _____, I feel _____.

Exercise 24: Organizing Your Feeling Word Vocabulary

Introduction

Having a feeling word chart will help you find feeling words as you practice responding to others.

Instructions

Record the new feeling words you generated in Exercise 23, or any other new feeling words you think of, on the next page.

Categories of Feelings

Levels of Intensity	Happy	Sad	Angry	Scared	Confused	Strong	Weak
HIGH	Excited Elated Joyful ____ ____ ____	Hopeless Depressed Devastated ____ ____ ____	Furious Livid Enraged ____ ____ ____	Fearful Afraid Threatened ____ ____ ____	Bewildered Trapped Lost ____ ____ ____	Passionate Resolute Unafraid ____ ____ ____	Overwhelmed Broken Vulnerable ____ ____ ____
MEDIUM	Cheerful Up Good ____ ____ ____	Upset Distressed Sorry ____ ____ ____	Agitated Frustrated Irritated ____ ____ ____	Worried Uneasy Hesitant ____ ____ ____	Disorganized Mixed-up Awkward ____ ____ ____	Energetic Confident Capable ____ ____ ____	Incapable Stressed Insecure ____ ____ ____
LOW	Glad Content Satisfied ____ ____ ____	Down Low Bad ____ ____ ____	Uptight Dismayed Annoyed ____ ____ ____	Timid Unsure Nervous ____ ____ ____	Bothered Uncomfortable Undecided ____ ____ ____	Sure Secure Solid ____ ____ ____	Lethargic Unsure Bored ____ ____ ____

The intensity of any feeling word depends upon the person with whom it is used. You will need to visualize the typical helpee you work with to categorize these words by intensity level. (An expanded word list is found in Appendix A of *The Art of Helping* 10th edition text.)

Exercise 25: Practicing Feeling Responses

Introduction

The next exercise will help you learn to select an appropriate feeling word and use that word in a response to feeling.

Instructions

Imagine that you are listening to each of the people listed below. Try to respond interchangeably to the feelings expressed by each. Use your feeling word chart or the feeling word list found in Appendix A of *The Art of Helping* text to find several words that fit the person.

Remember, the empathy question is, "How would I feel if I were this person?" not "How would I feel in that situation?"

Example:

Alcoholic: *"Things are all straightened out with my daughter now. I explained to her about my drinking problem and why I have to go to those long meetings. It's still hard for her 'cause she's so young, but she seems to understand that this is what I need to do to get well."*

1. You feel *relieved*

2. You feel *hopeful*

Exercise

1. **Student:** *"Here I am…again. It's mid-semester and I'm way behind in all my work and just barely passing a couple of courses. It's like I can't think ahead—one of the guys will come in and want to party and I say sure, then the next day I realize I didn't finish a paper or something. I do the same thing every semester. What's wrong with me— can't I learn from my past?"*

   a. You feel _____

   b. You feel _____

2. **Ex-wife:** *"My ex-husband is driving me crazy. We got a divorce six years ago and now suddenly he wants to fight me for custody of the kids. I know he doesn't have a case. I think he's harassing me just to get me mad."*

   a. You feel _____

   b. You feel _____

Exercise (continued)

3. **Middle School Student:** *"My best friend won't talk to me. During gym class she sat with my other friends and not with me. They were laughing a lot. I know they were talking about me."*

   a. You feel _____

   b. You feel _____

4. **Adult Male:** *"I'm just a three-quarters man. I've had so damn many opportunities in my life and I've thrown them all away."*

   a. You feel _____

   b. You feel _____

5. **Young Woman:** *"I'm really excited about my new job. I'm starting out at the bottom and the work is pretty dull right now, but there's so much to learn! The potential for advancement is really good."*

   a. You feel _____

   b. You feel _____

Exercise 26: More Feeling Response Practice

Introduction

This exercise provides more practice in responding to feelings.

Instructions

Write your best feeling response to each of the statements below. Use the format, *"You feel…,"* so that you have responses and not just a feeling word.

Example:

Adolescent Girl: *"My friends are pressuring me to do the same things they're doing. I don't want to smoke or drink, but I don't want to lose my friends either."*

Response to Feeling: *You feel trapped.*

Exercise

1. **Young Adult:** *"My friends tell me I'm very warm and outgoing and yet when I meet a new person, I'm uncomfortable and wonder what the new person is thinking about me."*

    Response to Feeling: _____

2. **Father:** *"I used to be a confident and happy person…before…my daughter was killed…and I just fell apart. I keep saying—if only I hadn't let her take the car that night. It was raining; she was just a kid; she just got her license. I should have driven her…now I've got to live with this. My daughter is gone, and I'm no longer the person I used to be."*

    Response to Feeling: _____

3. **Business Woman:** *"The new job is really working out. I have responsibilities for the supervision and training of our sales representatives. It's the right career path for me. I'm good at this and finally I'm getting the recognition and opportunity I've worked so hard to earn."*

    Response to Feeling: _____

4. **School Parent:** (Talking to school counselor): *"Thank you for meeting with me. My daughter showed me a disturbing conversation in her social media where a friend of hers talked about cutting herself. I don't want this girl to know that my daughter told me and that I told you, but I would feel awful if she did hurt herself, or worse, if I did not bring it to your attention."*

    Response to Feeling: _____

Exercise (continued)

5. **Teenager:** *"My mother is crazy. She yells at me all the time. No matter what I say or do, she finds a way to insult me. She never listens to me. She doesn't believe anything I say. I am always wrong and she is always right."*

    Response to Feeling: _____

6. **Parent:** *"I don't want my young adult son having sex with his girlfriend because of the chance of an unwanted pregnancy. On the one hand, my son is an adult and makes his own decisions. I realize that I need to keep my opinion to myself. But on the other hand, I want him to understand the risk and realize that he is gambling with his future, his girlfriend's future, and maybe the future of an unplanned new life."*

    Response to Feeling: _____

7. **Parent of Student:** *"I emailed my daughter's school counselor two days ago and have still not received a response. That is so unprofessional."*

    Response to Feeling: _____

8. **Teenager:** *"I lost my cool. I yelled at her and then I walked out. I should have had better control of my emotions."*

    Response to Feeling: _____

9. **Counselor:** *"I know that I cannot control another person's behavior. I can try to influence them, but in the end, they make their own decisions. All people are free to make their own choices."*

    Response to Feeling: _____

10. **Husband:** *"I couldn't have predicted my wife's reactions. I didn't say anything. It was my silence that set her off."*

    Response to Feeling: _____

Exercise 27: Practicing Responding to Two Feelings

Introduction

Sometimes a person will express two conflicting feelings. To respond effectively, you must be able to identify how the combination of the two feelings makes the person feel.

To respond to mixed feelings, you may find an accurate feeling word in the dominant feeling word category expressed by the helpee. In the "confused" feeling category, trust your life experiences. Ask yourself, "If I were this helpee and experiencing these conflicting emotions, how would I feel?"

Instructions

In the following responses, identify the two feelings present and then develop a response that accurately captures the whole feeling. To do this exercise successfully, ask yourself:

- *If I were this person, what word might best summarize my emotions if I felt _____ and _____.*

Now use this feeling word to formulate a response to the helpee:

- **Response:** *You feel _____.*

Example:

Parent: *"I don't want to fight with my kids all the time. I know I am responsible for giving them direction and helping them make wise decisions. But it is such a battle. Sometimes I feel like giving up."*

1. This parent feels <u>*responsible*</u> and <u>*exhausted*</u>.

2. **Response:** You feel <u>*discouraged*</u>.

Exercise

1. **Veteran:**   *"This position would give me decent money and health benefits. I think I should take it. But it doesn't really fit into my career plans and I'm not that interested in selling tires. Like you said, though, right now I need something to get me back on my feet and the job is good for that."*

   1. This veteran feels _____ and _____.

   2. **Response:** You feel _____.

Exercise (continued)

2. **Parent:** *"Our daughter has her first serious boyfriend. We're pleased that she's having the experience of developing a close relationship with a boyfriend, but we're not impressed by his work ethic or his life choices. Now we're in a difficult position."*

    1. This parent feels _____ and _____.

    2. **Response:** You feel _____.

3. **Young Adult:** *"I've been out of work for almost a year. Finally, I landed a good paying job. I like the work and especially the pay! The complication is that the job is second shift. That means I have to work every Monday through Friday 'till midnight. I mean, I can't play paying gigs with my musician buddies any evening, Monday through Friday. We've been playing out almost every weekend for the past 6 months. I enjoy it so much. I called in sick to work last Friday so I wouldn't miss a gig. But now I have to quit...something."*

    1. This young adult feels _____ and _____.

    2. **Response:** You feel _____.

4. **Professor:** *"It's difficult to tell whether to believe him or not. My gut impulse is that he's lying. His writing project just doesn't reflect him; the way he presents himself. If he didn't write his own paper, I can't let him get away with it. I'm suspicious, but I don't have any concrete evidence and I can't get this wrong."*

    1. This professor feels _____ and _____.

    2. **Response:** You feel _____.

5. **12-year-old:** *"My Mom is sick all the time. The doctors don't know what's wrong. My Dad is out of work. We might have to move if Dad doesn't get back to work soon because we won't be able to pay the mortgage. There's nothing I can do about any of this."*

    1. This child feels _____ and _____.

    2. **Response:** You feel _____.

Responding to Meaning

Overview

A response to meaning communicates an understanding of the full experience of the helpee: an understanding of both the feeling and the reason for it. We call this, *"You feel _____ because _____"* response to meaning, an interchangeable response.

Dorm Resident:	*"I just don't understand it. I walked into my room this afternoon and my roommate totally ignored me! I asked her what was wrong, she looked at me and said, 'You should know," then left. What am I supposed to do if she doesn't let me in on what's bothering her?"*
Response:	*"You feel bewildered because your roommate is not giving you any clues as to why she's so upset."*

This response combines the two responses you have already practiced, responding to content and to feeling. Review *The Art of Helping,* pages 133–140 for an explanation of this skill.

Exercise 28: Discriminating Interchangeable Responses

Introduction

If you have the ability to recognize good (helpful) and bad (unhelpful) responses, you will be able to give yourself feedback on your own future responses and improve your responding skills.

Instructions

Select the response that is interchangeable for each statement. When a response is *not* interchangeable, identify an error in the response.

Remember, some typical errors are:

➢ Content **too long** (keep responses brief)

➢ Content **parroted** (paraphrase your responses)

➢ Content too **vague** (be specific)

➢ Feeling **category** inaccurate

➢ Feeling **intensity** inaccurate

➢ Feeling work **inappropriate** for the person being responded to

➢ Feeling **experience** is described ("you feel that…", or "you feel like…", but no feeling **word** is included)

➢ Content **not interchangeable** (adds or subtracts content, judgmental)

Example:

Job Hunter: *"Many employers want managers to be micro-managers. They believe that you're sup-posed to track employees all the time. I'm just not that way."*

a. You feel annoyed because many employers require a management practice of close control over employees and you don't agree with that approach.

Error(s): *None. This is an interchangeable response.*

b. You feel good because you are different.

Error(s): *Wrong feeling category; content too vague (not interchangeable)*

c. You feel sore because no one will hire you as a manager.

Error(s): *Wrong feeling intensity; adds content that the job hunter did not state (not interchangeable)*

d. You feel like you're being blocked because many employers won't like you.

Error(s): *No feeling word. Content too vague (not interchangeable)*

e. You feel discouraged because the business world does not actually appreciate creativity.

Error(s): *Adds content (not interchangeable)*

Exercise

1. **Boss:** *"I'm fed up! No one around here takes me seriously. The next person who comes in late is fired...and I mean it."*

    a. You feel **mad** because **employees are no good these days.**

    Error: _____

    _____

    b. You feel **irritated** because **people don't pay any attention to what you say.**

    Error: _____

    _____

    c. You feel **confused** because **the people here don't listen to you.**

    Error: _____

    _____

    d. You feel **angry** because **of this.**

    Error: _____

    _____

    e. You feel **embarrassed** because **people don't believe you'll act on what you threaten.**

    Error: _____

    _____

Exercise (continued)

2. **Seamstress:** *"Hey, this is really excellent. The quality of this material is exactly what I've been looking for. Now I can finish the suit I designed."*

    a. You feel that **the material is perfect for your suit.**

    Error: _____

    _____

    b. You feel **pleased** about this.

    Error: _____

    _____

    c. You feel **thrilled** because **the quality of the material is excellent and exactly what you've been looking for.** Now you can finish the suit you designed.

    Error: _____

    _____

    d. You feel **hopeful** because **this material is of such high quality.** It's quite excellent material and because the material is so good, you can complete the suit you've been working on. You've been looking for material like this, so it's really great to find it.

    Error: _____

    _____

    e. You feel **happy** because **the material is excellent for completing your suit.**

    Error: _____

    _____

(Exercise 28 answers are on page 181.)

Exercise 29: Practicing Responding to Meaning (Practicing Making Interchangeable Responses)

Introduction

This exercise gives you time to generate a quality response to meaning. Writing your responses will help you build experience for the future when you will need to respond verbally and "in-the-moment."

Interchangeable responses to meaning communicate the helpee's feeling and an external reason for this feeling. If you find that your best response naturally requires the inclusion of the word "you" after the word "because," then you are making a personalized response to meaning. When you add the word "you" to follow "because," the words that follow will communicate the helpee's ownership or role in the situation. When accurate, those will be great responses!

At this time, refrain from using the word "you" after "because" so you can practice making interchangeable responses. Interchangeable responses to meaning describe "external" reasons for the helpee's feelings and are the easiest for the helpees to accept as accurate. An interchangeable response to meaning will externalize blame or causality for the situation to someone or something else. Here is an example of an interchangeable response; one that externalizes responsibility:

> **Helper:** "You feel **angry** because **the teacher's policy is unfair.**
>
> (In this case, "the teacher's policy" is the external reason for the helpee's angry feeling.)

Coming soon! Within a few pages you will be learning and practicing formulating personalized responses to meaning where you will add the word "you" after the word "because" and facilitate the helpees to take ownership or responsibility for their role in their situation.

Instructions

Write your best responses to each of the statements below using the format:

"You feel _____ because _____."

Example:

> **Husband:** "Two days ago, my wife told me that our marriage is over. She said that she's dissatisfied with her life with me and needs to find meaning in her life. I'm beyond hurt."
>
> **Response:** *You feel devastated because your wife is breaking up your marriage.*

Exercise

1. **Dorm Resident:** *"My roommate is such a selfish person. I don't think he ever had to think of anyone else in his life—everything in our room is organized his way."*

   Response: _____

   _____

2. **Friend:** *"I think she's going nuts. Last night, out of the blue, she sent everyone home. I mean, nothing happened; it was just suddenly she wanted to be alone."*

   Response: _____

   _____

3. **Young Driver:** *"My Aunt and Uncle are about to purchase a new car. Today, they called to offer me their old car at no cost! It's a nice car too!"*

   Response: _____

   _____

4. **Young Adult:** *"I graduated from high school last year. I'm handling a college course load. I work a summer job. I'm an adult, but my parents won't let my girlfriend stay overnight with me. I know it's their house, but it's my life."*

   Response: _____

   _____

5. **Ticketed Driver:** *"I was caught in a 'speed trap.' Now I'm out $125 for the fine and court costs. The road was straight and should have been posted as a 45 mph speed limit. Instead, it's posted at 30. I didn't notice the sign. When I drive, I read the road. My experience tells me how fast I can safely drive. Who set up that speed trap? That person is a criminal, not me."*

   Response: _____

   _____

6. **Pot Smoker:** *"I work in a pressure-cooker environment. It's non-stop. Everything is due 'now' or even 'yesterday'." Every day, as soon as I get out of work, I need to smoke a joint to calm down."*

   Response: _____

   _____

Exercise (continued)

7. **Worker:** *"Recognition for quality work is not acknowledged in my work group. We do the heavy lifting and my boss takes all the credit."*

   Response: _____

   _____

8. **Airline Passenger:** *"I've been standing in line for about 45 minutes, waiting to get through security. I might miss my flight. There are two sets of machinery for checking passengers and their carry-ons, but only one is open. Why? The guy in front of me loudly asked the workers to open a second line. One of the workers approached and would not provide any information beyond disrespectfully stating that we 'just have to wait, period'."*

   Response: _____

   _____

9. **Client:** *"Your advice was bad. I went in and told my supervisor how I thought he could become more productive. He said that I should stick to my own work and keep my nose out of his business."*

   Response: _____

   _____

10. **Husband:** *"My wife told me that our marriage is over. She said that she's dissatisfied with her life and needs to find herself. I think her idealistic friends put this 'search for meaning' idea into her head. That's the only way I can explain this. We've been married for 18 years and have two great kids. How can she let herself be influenced by these mid-life crisis, divorced friends?"*

   Response: _____

   _____

Exercise 30: Responding to Yourself

Introduction

Up to this point, you have been practicing with a variety of helpee statements—but no live helpees. To help you make the transition from these written helpee statements to a live person, the following exercise will give you a chance to help yourself.

Responding to yourself will give you an opportunity to begin working with a live helpee whom you know very well. Familiarity makes responding easier. You will also get an idea of what it is like to be a helpee.

Instructions

1a. Write a brief paragraph describing some current experience in your life as a learner.

_____

_____

_____

_____

_____

_____

_____

_____

_____

_____

_____

_____

1b. Respond to how you feel and why.

I feel _____ because _____

_____

Instructions (continued)

2a. Write a brief paragraph describing something going on in your home or social life.

_____

_____

_____

_____

_____

_____

_____

_____

_____

2b. Respond to how you feel and why.

I feel _____ because _____

_____

3a. Write a brief paragraph describing something you would like to change in your work setting. (If you are not currently employed, describe some other situation that you would like to change.)

_____

_____

_____

_____

_____

_____

_____

_____

3b. Respond to how you feel and why.

I feel _____ because _____

_____

❹ Personalizing: Facilitating Helpee Understanding

Overview

You have learned to attend to another person's experience by attending physically, observing, and listening. You have also learned to respond accurately and interchangeably to the feeling and content that the other person expressed. Now you will learn to *personalize* the person's experience.

Personalizing involves building an interchangeable base, personalizing meaning, personalizing the problem, personalizing the goal, and personalizing changing feelings so the person can identify where he or she is in relation to where he or she wants to be. An example of the personalizing process is given below. The exercises following it will take you through each step of personalizing.

Before you do any of these exercises, read Chapter 6 of *The Art of Helping* text (pages 147–213) to learn about personalizing.

Example:

The following dialogue illustrates the steps of personalizing.

Building an Interchangeable Base

Patient:	*"No one's told me a thing. I feel like I'm just a disease lying here! No one treats me like they see me!"*
Response:	You feel annoyed because the people here ignore you.
Patient:	*"Ignore me? They avoid me! I'm not even aware of what's wrong with me. If I paid attention to the way they treat me, I'd think I had leprosy."*
Response:	You feel angry because they act like it'll harm them to approach you.
Patient:	*It wouldn't take much. A little decency. I don't want them to betray information...I just want to be seen...and spoken to."*
Response:	You feel lonely because no one talks to you.
Patient:	*"I've been here in this hospital ward two weeks now and it's like living in prison—cold and sterile, being all alone with no control."*
Response:	You feel anxious because the staff is in charge—totally.
Patient:	*"If I just knew what was wrong. They clam up when they're around me and it's scaring me. What does it mean?"*
Response:	You feel frightened because they seem to be hiding something bad from you.

Example (continued)

Patient:	*"I had this real bad pain in my head and then seemed to black out. So my family brought me in. We were scared...a brain tumor? The doctor says 'no'...but what?"*
Response:	You feel lost because there hasn't been a clear diagnosis.

Personalized Meaning

Patient:	*"I try to ask, but I get overwhelmed by worry and I freeze. (pause) Maybe I'm happier not knowing. But I wish I knew—it's my body, maybe my life."*
Response:	You feel scared because you're left not knowing what's going on.
Patient:	*"And I don't know why I don't just ask the doctor outright. I'm stuck. I don't think that I can overcome this fear. What if I can't handle the bad news?"*
Response:	You feel afraid because you believe that you might "fall apart" emotionally if the doctor's news is real bad.

Personalized Problem

Patient:	*"Yeah, I'm terrified...and my terror keeps me ignorant! I'm feeling like I'm just lying here awaiting doom."*
Response:	You feel vulnerable because you can't act unless you know what's wrong and, right now, you can't get the information from your doctor that you need.

Personalized Problem

Patient:	*"I can't act, I can't even get up the nerve to ask the doc to tell me the truth."*
Response:	You feel frustrated with yourself because you can't ask the doctor what's wrong.

Personalized Goal

Patient:	*"And it's making me sicker. I'm scared...(pause) but I've got to find out."*
Response:	You feel desperate because you can't help yourself without the information and you know that you need to ask the doctor what's wrong with you.

Personalized Meaning

Patient:	*"Yeah, I do...I have to. I need to prepare myself for what he might say...Even if it's bad news, I'll get some relief just knowing."*
Response:	You feel anxious to find out because your knowing may lead to some sense of relief from the terror of the unknown.

Exercise 31: Exploring Personalizing Skills

Introduction

This exercise will help you to understand the importance of personalizing skills for effective helping.

Instructions

Think back to the last time that someone gave you some information that helped you to understand what you needed to do to solve a problem. Then, answer the following questions.

Exercises

1. Who was the helpful person and what was the problem?

   _____

   _____

   _____

   _____

   _____

   _____

   _____

   _____

2. Did the person help you to *identify your role in the situation?*

   ☐ Yes   ☐ No

3. Did the person help you to *see what you were doing or not doing that made the problem worse?*

   ☐ Yes   ☐ No

4. Did you *have a goal after talking to this person?*

   ☐ Yes   ☐ No

5. Why are the following helper attributes important?

   a. Shows you that your point of view was understood

   _____

   _____

   _____

   _____

Exercises (continued)

b. Helps you to identify your role in the situation

_____

_____

_____

_____

c. Helps you to identify what you were doing or not doing that made the problem worse

_____

_____

_____

_____

d. Helps you to develop a goal

_____

_____

_____

_____

6. What was it about the person or your relationship to him or her that made you accept and use the information that he or she gave you?

_____

_____

_____

_____

_____

_____

_____

_____

Personalizing Meaning

Overview

When helpees talk about how other people and outside events impact their lives, they are *externalizing* responsibility for their experiences. "They did this to me!" When helpees talk about themselves, about what they are doing or not doing, about the impact of their behaviors, or about why they are feeling and acting the way they are, they are *internalizing* the meaning of their experiences. "Here is what I am doing that is contributing to this situation."

The skill of personalizing meaning involves assisting helpees to internalize or take ownership of:

- their behaviors and **experiences**,
- the results or **implications** of their behaviors, and
- their **assumptions** or reasons for their behaviors.

Personalized meaning responses may be formulated and communicated to add to the helpees' understanding of the helpees' experiences and their participation in these experiences, the implications or consequences of their roles in their experiences, and the helpees' understanding or their assumptions or beliefs about their situations.

To check your understanding of personalizing meaning, review *The Art of Helping* text, pages 152–155 and 159–169.

Example:

Entrepreneur: *"I've got some terrific ideas for starting a new business. But my bankers won't give me a loan to get started. I made a presentation, but they don't value ideas. They only value things like real estate and cash. They don't understand me, but I will try other bankers and other investors."*

Interchangeable Response to Meaning
(Externalizing Responsibility)

You feel upset because your bankers are being so narrow-minded.

Note: The interchangeable response communicates externalized responsibility. "The bankers," not the helpee, are the cause or reason for the helpee feeling upset.

Personalized Meaning
(Internalizing Experience)

You feel annoyed because you tell a story that is clear and meaningful to you but is misunderstood and misjudged by the bankers you have met.

Note: The focus of this personalized response to meaning internalizes and makes personal the helpee's actions and experience. This response adds to what the helpee has stated and expands the helpee's understanding of his/her experience.

Example (continued)

Personalized Meaning
(Internalizing Assumptions)

> You feel confident because you believe that you will find a way to obtain the necessary financing.
>
> **Note:** The focus of this personalized response to meaning expands the helpee's understanding of his/her assumptions or beliefs about his/her behavior.

Building upon an interchangeable base of communication, we begin to assist our helpees to understand their experiences at increasingly deeper levels. We patiently hear them externalizing responsibility for their situations. Now, with personalized meaning responses, we insert the word "you" after the word "because" and assist our helpees to reveal or discover deeper levels of understanding of their behaviors and experiences; the implications of their behaviors; and even their undergirding life-assumptions or beliefs.

Personalizing meaning provides a foundation of understanding upon which we will assist our helpees to then define their problems and goals.

Exercise 32: Discriminating Personalized Meaning Responses

Introduction

Personalized meaning responses assist helpees to expand their thinking about their situations and help them better understand their personal connection to their situations. Personalized Responses to Meaning can be about the helpees' **experiences,** the **implications** or effects of the helpees' experiences, or the **assumptions** or beliefs of the helpees.

Instructions

Read the helpee stimulus statement. Then read each of the following four helper statements. For each helper statement, identify if it is:

- **IR** – an Interchangeable Response to Meaning,

- **PM (Experience)** – a Personalized Response to Meaning about the helpee's experience,

- **PM (Implications)** – a Personalized Response to Meaning about the implications for the helpee, or

- **PM (Assumptions)** – a Personalized Response to Meaning about the assumptions or beliefs of the helpee.

Exercise

| **High School Student:** | *"My English class is awful. We're required to read books with storylines about child abuse, genocide, mental illness, death by drug overdose, stroke, and life on a heart and lung machine. Can't we read and write about some happy topics too?"* |

TYPE OF RESPONSE

1. _____ You're annoyed because the required reading is all about depressing topics.

2. _____ You feel burdened because you have to read, think, and write about so many emotionally heavy issues.

3. _____ You feel disappointed because you're not able to use this time to read and write about more enjoyable topics.

4. _____ You feel resentful because you are once again forced to give up your right to make choices for yourself and find this to be unfair.

(Exercise 32 answers are on page 181.)

Exercise 33: Formulating Personalized Meaning Responses

Introduction

Personalized meaning responses are both empathic and additive. These responses are empathic because they communicate the helpee's experience, the implications of the helpee's behavior, and the helpee's assumptions or beliefs. These responses are additive when the helper expands the helpee's understanding by introducing useful information that is accurate and but has not been explicitly stated by the helpee.

Instructions

This exercise begins with a statement from the helpee. For practice purposes, a single helpee statement is provided to stimulate you to formulate and write four different responses. As a helper in a real-life situation, you would probably formulate and deliver a single response, listen to what the helpee has to say, and then follow with another response. With each response, the helper will stay finely tuned to the helpee's needs for a deeper understanding of the helpee's experience and behaviors, implications of helpee behaviors, and any need to discuss helpee assumptions or beliefs. (After completing this exercise, turn to page 84 to see how one experienced helper responded to this exercise.)

Exercise

1a. **Drug Addict:** *"I have a disease. I'm an addict. While most of the people I grew up with are in college or working, I'm high every day. I had talents and dreams, but now I'm wasted and wasting away."*

Interchangeable Response to Meaning (Externalizing Responsibility)

You feel _____

because _____

_____

Personalized Meaning (Internalizing Experience)

You feel _____

because you _____

_____

Personalized Meaning (Internalizing Implications)

You feel _____

because you _____

_____

Personalized Meaning (Internalizing Assumptions)

You feel _____

because you _____

_____

Exercise (continued)

Here is how one experienced helper responded to the exercise on the previous page.

1b. **Drug Addict:** *"I have a disease. I'm an addict. While most of the people I grew up with are in college or working, I'm high every day. I had talents and dreams, but now I'm wasted and wasting away."*

Interchangeable Response to Meaning (Externalizing Responsibility)

You feel _angry_

because _your drug habits are in control._

Personalized Meaning (Internalizing Experience)

You feel _trapped_

because you _find yourself living a pattern you did not intend to live._

Personalized Meaning (Internalizing Implications)

You feel _depressed_

because you _know that you're missing out on educational, social, and economic opportunities._

Personalized Meaning (Internalizing Assumptions)

You feel _vulnerable_

because you _have lost confidence in your ability to control your life choices._

Exercise (continued)

Formulate and write each of the four difference responses requested.

2a. **Husband:** *"She asked me to leave. We're separated now. Things just slipped away without either of us noticing. (pause) I'm losing a part of myself. It's sad how little time we give to what matters most. I don't know if we can repair our marriage; be close again. But I haven't given up hope."*

Interchangeable Response to Meaning (Externalizing Responsibility)

You feel _____

because _____

Personalized Meaning (Internalizing Experience)

You feel _____

because you _____

Personalized Meaning (Internalizing Implications)

You feel _____

because you _____

Personalized Meaning (Internalizing Assumptions)

You feel _____

because you _____

Exercise (continued)

Here is how one experienced helper responded to the exercise on the previous page.

2b. **Husband:** *"She asked me to leave. We're separated now. Things just slipped away without either of us noticing. (pause) I'm losing a part of myself. It's sad how little time we give to what matters most. I don't know if we can repair our marriage; be close again. But I haven't given up hope."*

Interchangeable Response to Meaning (Externalizing Responsibility)

You feel   *crushed*

because   *she decided to break up your marriage.*

Personalized Meaning (Internalizing Experience)

You feel   *regretful*

because you   *wish you would have noticed that the two of you were growing apart.*

Personalized Meaning (Internalizing Implications)

You feel   *lost*

because you   *are experiencing a painful void living without her.*

Personalized Meaning (Internalizing Assumptions)

You feel   *hopeful that your marriage might be able to be renewed*

because you   *aren't yet willing to give up this hope.*

Personalizing Problems

Overview

Personalizing a problem requires identifying what a person *cannot do* that is contributing to their problem.

Example:

Sister: *"They talk about my sister like she isn't there. It really bothers me when I don't interfere. I'm older; I could protect her. I want to do it right, though and I never know what to say, how to handle it."*

Personalized Problem:

You feel *badly* **because you cannot** *handle the people who mistreat your sister.*

Review pages 175–185 in *The Art of Helping* text before doing the following exercises.

Exercise 34: Discriminating Personalized Problem Responses

Introduction

In this exercise, you will practice discriminating personalized problem **(PP)** responses from personalized meaning **(PM)** responses and interchangeable responses **(IR)** to meaning.

Instructions

Read the statements and responses in the exercise that follows and identify the responses using the following scale:

> **PP** – Personalized Problem
> **PM** – Personalized Meaning
> **IR** – Interchangeable Response

Example:

Middle-Aged Husband: *"I know I've got to handle this myself. It really gets me down, watching my wife return to drinking. But I can't join her. I've got to be strong enough to say no. It's my only chance—and if I can beat it, maybe I can help her beat her alcoholism."*

IR	a.	You feel sad because your wife is destroying herself.
PM	b.	You feel alone because you're the only one you can count on.
PP	c.	You feel inadequate because you cannot help your wife before you help yourself.

Exercise

1. **Young Adult:** *"I guess when I was a teenager, I felt down all the time and the 'speed' made me feel better. But now, the drug is running me; I'm out of control and yet I keep on taking it."*

   _____ a. You feel scared because you cannot break your drug habit.

   _____ b. You feel uneasy because the "speed" is in control.

   _____ c. You feel helpless because you've given up control of your life.

2. **Lower Management Employee:** *"They really use me in that store. I do everything and I just don't think anybody notices. I'm not recognized because I don't fit in. I'm too unique; that's what it is. And I speak up when things seem wrong to me; I have to. Upper management doesn't want the interpersonal friction that results from my honest feedback. They'll never promote me."*

   _____ a. You feel irritated because they don't appreciate your value to them.

   _____ b. You feel discouraged because you don't fit what they're looking for.

   _____ c. You feel frustrated because you cannot get promoted when you voice your own opinion the way you do.

3. **21-year-old:** *"My boyfriend wants me to live with him. He keeps mentioning it and I keep saying no. I'm not really sure why not...and so I can't make it clear to him. He gets hurt...disappointed. I don't want that to happen, but I know I'm not ready to live with him."*

   _____ a. You feel conflicted because you aren't sure of your reasons for saying no.

   _____ b. You feel bad because he gets disappointed by your refusal.

   _____ c. You feel distressed because you can't explain—or don't fully understand—what you want for yourself.

Exercise (continued)

4. **30-year-old Husband:** *"I don't know what I want to do with my marriage. I want to be fair to my wife, but I don't know if I love her or not. It's unfair for both of us. I'm half married, half single."*

_____ a. You feel depressed because you can't decide whether to make a commitment to your marriage or get out.

_____ b. You feel disoriented because your marriage is so unsettled.

_____ c. You feel guilty because you know that you're cheating your wife, your marriage, and yourself by your indecision.

(Exercise 34 answers are on page 181.)

Exercise 35: Practicing Personalizing Problems

Introduction

Now you are ready to formulate personalized problem responses of your own.

Instructions

Write three responses to each helpee excerpt:

1. Write an interchangeable response to meaning
2. Write a response to the personalized meaning
3. Write a response to the personalized problem

Example:

Young Man: *"This diet doesn't work either. I've been trying to lose weight for, well, it seems like forever. I get excited every time I start a new diet, but I never stay with it. Even if I lose some weight I can't keep it off."*

1. **Interchangeable Response:**

   You feel   *discouraged*

   because   *the diets don't work.*

2. **Personalized Meaning:**

   You feel   *frustrated*

   because you   *don't stay on your diets.*

3. **Personalized Problem:**

   You feel   *disappointed*

   because you cannot   *find a way to lose weight permanently.*

Exercise

1. **Parent:** *"My son is at it again. He's 32 and has a family of his own. He can't stop drinking booze. His wife tossed him out and he's been staying with us. He's been drinking here too. He denies it, but we know it's true. We're not young anymore. What can we do?"*

   a. **Interchangeable Response:**

   You feel _____

   because _____

   b. **Personalized Meaning:**

   You feel _____

   because you _____

   c. **Personalized Problem:**

   You feel _____

   because you cannot _____

2. **Employee:** *"I did it again! I blew it again! I just don't seem to be able to think before I open my big mouth. This job was going so smoothly before I got mad and told off my supervisor."*

   a. **Interchangeable Response:**

   You feel _____

   because _____

   b. **Personalized Meaning:**

   You feel _____

   because you _____

   c. **Personalized Problem:**

   You feel _____

   because you cannot _____

Exercise (continued)

3. **Psychiatric Patient:** *"This staff is keeping me a prisoner here. I just want to go home. They tell me that I'm not thinking clearly and that they're trying to figure out why. What they mean is that they think I'm crazy. Am I crazy? I'd like to know. Wouldn't you?"*

   a. **Interchangeable Response:**

     You feel _____

     because _____

   b. **Personalized Meaning:**

     You feel _____

     because you _____

   c. **Personalized Problem:**

     You feel _____

     because you cannot _____

4. **Wife:** *"I'm hurt. I gave 25 years to my marriage with him and now it's over. I feel cheated. I'm an old woman now. I thought my life would be settled at this point. I never expected to be starting over. It hurts so much…I don't know if I can even do it."*

   a. **Interchangeable Response:**

     You feel _____

     because _____

   b. **Personalized Meaning:**

     You feel _____

     because you _____

   c. **Personalized Problem:**

     You feel _____

     because you cannot _____

Personalizing Goals

Overview

Personalizing the goal is the step that establishes where the helpee wants to be in relation to where he or she is. Before completing the next three exercises, review pages 186–195 of *The Art of Helping* text.

Exercise 36: Discriminating Personalized Goal Behavior

Introduction

This exercise will help you learn to identify whether or not the goal is consistent with and appropriate for the problem. Goal behavior can be defined as the **flip-side** of the problem behavior.

Instructions

Read the helpee excerpt, then read each of the helper responses. Each helper response is an attempt to personalize a goal for the helpee. As you will see, the first half of the response is a description of the helpee's problem. The second half of the response is a description of the helpee's goal. Effective personalized goals flow directly from the personalized problem. They are the *flip-side* of the problem. In other words, the second half of the response is the *flip-side* of the first half of the response. Ineffective personalized goals do not flow directly from the personalized problem. Instead, they introduce new behaviors.

To complete the exercise, label each response according to how the goal was developed: *flip-side* (effective goal—directly related to the description of the problem) or new behavior (ineffective goal—not directly related to the description of the problem).

Example:

High School Athlete: *"You never give me a chance. You always pick someone else. You don't value me."*

You feel discouraged because you can't find a way to be a part of the group and you want to belong.

      ☑ Flip-side   ☐ New Behavior

You feel discouraged because you can't find a way to be a part of the group and you need to open up more.

      ☐ Flip-side   ☑ New Behavior

Exercise

1. **High School Math Student:** *"I try to hard to keep up in class. I do all the homework and everything. But the stuff is way above my head."*

   a. You feel worried because you can't do the work and you want to be able to be better prepared for your next test.

   ☐ Flip-side ☐ New Behavior

   b. You feel helpless because you can't handle the material and you want very much to be able to manage it.

   ☐ Flip-side ☐ New Behavior

   c. You feel upset because you can't learn this subject and you really want to be enrolled in an easier course.

   ☐ Flip-side ☐ New Behavior

2. **Worker:** *"I don't know if I want this new job. The money's better, but I'd have to deal with a whole different group of people who might not give me the support that I have here."*

   a. You feel vulnerable because you don't have the responses to support yourself in a new job with new people and you want to learn those responses.

   ☐ Flip-side ☐ New Behavior

   b. You feel unsure because you can't decide about the new job and you want to make a decision you'll feel good about.

   ☐ Flip-side ☐ New Behavior

   c. You feel lost because you can't deal with new people effectively and you want to be able to accept the new job offer.

   ☐ Flip-side ☐ New Behavior

Exercise (continued)

3. **Employee:** *"I'm so angry. First they tell me one thing, then they change the rules. I just don't seem to be able to say 'enough is enough'."*

    a.   You feel disappointed because you can't end the game-playing and you want to learn how to be a winner for a change.

       ☐ Flip-side   ☐ New Behavior

    b.   You feel disgusted with yourself because you can't take a firm stand and you want to be able to.

       ☐ Flip-side   ☐ New Behavior

    c.   You feel angry with yourself because you can't stand up for your rights and you need to learn to stay out of situations where you will not be treated justly.

       ☐ Flip-side   ☐ New Behavior

4. **Young Husband:** *"My wife is always nagging. Nothing I do is right anymore. It's complain if I come home late and complain if I come home early, and forbid the thought that I should mention her shortcomings!"*

    a.   You feel sad because you don't know how to break out of the destructive pattern you're in and you want to break the cycle.

       ☐ Flip-side   ☐ New Behavior

    b.   You feel helpless because you can't get your wife to understand you and you want to be able to do what you want.

       ☐ Flip-side   ☐ New Behavior

    c.   You feel trapped because you can't communicate with your wife anymore and you really want to be able to talk with one another again.

       ☐ Flip-side   ☐ New Behavior

(Exercise 36 answers are on page 182.)

Exercise 37: Discriminating Personalized Goals

Introduction

In the following exercise, you will practice discriminating interchangeable responses (IR) to meaning, personalized meaning (PM) responses, personalized problem (PP) responses, and personalized goal (PG) responses.

Instructions

After the following excerpts, you will find five responses. Read each response and identify what type of response it is. Label all five responses. Each response will be one of the following:

1. **IR** – Interchangeable Response to meaning:

   "You feel _____ because _____."

2. **PM** – Personalized Meaning:

   "You feel _____ because you _____."

3. **PP** – Personalized Problem:

   "You feel _____ because you cannot _____."

4. **PG** – Personalized Goal:

   "You feel _____ because you cannot _____

   and you want to _____."

Example:

28-year-old Woman: *"All my life I've felt like I was searching for something. I know I'm a good person; I'm decent. I should be satisfied with myself. But there's a sense of something missing. I'm not who I could be. I'm not complete somehow."*

RESPONSE

_____*IR*_____ 1. You feel dissatisfied because some essential experience is still absent from your life and what it is remains a mystery.

_____*PM*_____ 2. You feel angry with yourself because you have lost so much time.

_____*PM*_____ 3. You feel sad because you might have lived your life differently if you'd had this missing information.

_____*PP*_____ 4. You feel weak inside because you cannot define what is missing.

_____*PG*_____ 5. You feel disappointed because you haven't yet determined what it is that is missing in your life and you want deeply to find it.

Exercise

1. **High School Girl:** *"It's really good talking to you like this. Usually, I can't talk with people my age. I'm self-conscious and uneasy. I feel like I don't belong. I'm different from most young people. I'd love to be social and relaxed, but I know I'm not one of them. They know it too, and they stay away from me."*

   RESPONSE

   _____ a. You feel sad because people aren't friendly with you.

   _____ b. You feel alone because people your age never welcome you as a friend.

   _____ c. You feel unhappy because you have not made any friends.

   _____ d. You feel alone because you cannot get along with people your age.

   _____ e. You feel disappointed in yourself because you cannot relate to people your age and you want to be able to relate to them.

2. **Politician:** *"My whole life has been this way. Every time I get an opportunity to do something, I seem to ruin it. I make terrible decisions, do dumb things, lose my temper...it's like I get scared and...deliberately ruin my chances."*

   RESPONSE

   _____ a. You feel angry because you destroy your opportunities.

   _____ b. You feel frustrated because you have a track record of self-inflicted failures.

   _____ c. You feel disgusted with yourself because you act impulsively and cannot act strategically.

   _____ d. You feel depressed because opportunities are easily lost.

   _____ e. You feel angry at yourself because you cannot control your actions and you want to be able to control your impulsive behavior.

Exercise (continued)

3. **Professional Woman:** *"My husband is a decent person, but he's kind of a 'mama's boy'—his family always takes precedence. It's annoying. I don't know if we should have ever gotten married. Lately, I just seem unhappy. And I work with so many attractive and interesting men. I get conflicted. Why can't I settle down with the man I have?"*

   RESPONSE

   _____ a. You feel disoriented because you cannot control your interest in other men.

   _____ b. You feel confused because you cannot make up your mind about how you feel and you want to settle this internal conflict.

   _____ c. You feel insecure because you keep looking for something...somebody... who's more than your husband.

   _____ d. You feel angry at yourself because you cannot make an unconflicted commitment to your husband.

   _____ e. You feel cheated because your husband never outgrew his childhood priorities.

4. **Mother:** *"I don't want to fight with my kids all the time. I know that I'm responsible for giving them direction and helping them make wise decisions, but it is such a battle. Sometimes I feel like giving up."*

   RESPONSE

   _____ a. You feel discouraged because raising kids is such a struggle.

   _____ b. You feel anxious because you don't want to fail them.

   _____ c. You feel disappointed with yourself because you don't always give your kids the constructive direction that they need.

   _____ d. You feel stuck because you can't relate to your kids without it turning into an argument and you want your communication with them to be positive, not a confrontation.

   _____ e. You feel exhausted because you can't keep up with your kids.

(Exercise 37 answers are on page 182.)

Exercise 38: Practicing Personalizing Goals

Introduction

In this exercise you will practice writing responses that personalize problems and goals.

Remember, a good personalized goal is the flip-side of the problem and does not introduce a new behavior.

Instructions

Write a personalized problem and personalized goal response for each of the following statements.

Example:

Woman: *"I feel so guilty. I was sober for 18 months and I thought I had it all together. Then the tension got to me; I just feel apart and went back to drinking again."*

    1. **Personalize the problem:** *You feel discouraged with yourself because you* *can't handle the tension without the booze.*

    2. **Personalize the goal:** *You feel discouraged because you can't handle stress* *without drinking and you want to learn constructive ways of dealing with stress.*

Exercise

    1. **35-year-old Woman:** *"That bastard! He was beating me up so I divorced him. Then I had to get a restraining order to keep him away. He left me alone 'till he heard I had a new boyfriend and was putting my life back together. As soon as he heard that, he came back and beat up my boyfriend."*

        a. **Personalize the problem:** You feel _____

        because you cannot _____

        _____

        b. **Personalize the goal:** You feel _____

        because you cannot _____

        _____ and you want to _____

        _____

Exercise (continued)

2. **Parent:** *"We tried so hard with him. We knew he had lots of problems so we tried to make it easy for him. I guess we were too easy when he was growing up. He has just taken and taken and taken from us. We've got to get him out of the house, for our own sanity."*

    a. **Personalize the problem:** You feel _____

    because you cannot _____

    _____

    b. **Personalize the goal:** You feel _____

    because you cannot _____

    _____ and you want to _____

    _____

3. **33-year-old Woman:** *"I don't know quite how to say this, but...uh...whenever...uh...my husband wants to go to...go to bed with me, I just feel sick. I feel disgusted. I have to grit my teeth and think of the kid's welfare...If I don't...uh...sleep with him, he'll leave me."*

    a. **Personalize the problem:** You feel _____

    because you cannot _____

    _____

    b. **Personalize the goal:** You feel _____

    because you cannot _____

    _____ and you want to _____

    _____

Exercise (continued)

4. **Father:** *"I'm so worried about my daughter. She's had three nervous breakdowns in two years. Her husband's an alcoholic and beats her. I'm just sick. She refuses to leave him and her mental state is getting worse and worse."*

    a. **Personalize the problem:** You feel _____

       because you cannot _____

       _____

    b. **Personalize the goal:** You feel _____

       because you cannot _____

       _____ and you want to _____

       _____

Personalizing Changing Feelings

Overview

Personalizing changing feelings means being attuned to helpee emotions as they move from the despair of their current situation to hope for a better future.

Exercise 39: Practicing Personalizing Feelings

Introduction

When helpees communicate how they feel about their responsibility for how they currently handle their problems, they usually note a *disappointment* in themselves. When helpees communicate how they feel about their goals, they usually note some *optimism,* as they can now see a way out of their problems. It is essential that helpers stay tuned to the helpee's changing feelings.

Instructions

Read the following helpee excerpts and then write a personalized response to feeling. Be sure to stay tuned to the helpees' feelings about their problems and goals.

Example:

Young Woman: *"You're so…together. I look at you and say, 'How does she do it?' You're not much older. But when I compare myself to you…I still live at home; I depend on my parents for everything. I feel like a kid next to you."*

Personalized Feeling (about problem): You feel   *disappointed with yourself*

because you   *can't live independently.*

Young Woman: **After defining a goal:** *"Within 6 months, I could have my own car and I would be a lot more independent!"*

Personalized Feeling (about goal):   You feel   *optimistic now*

because you   *see a way to take charge of your own movement toward independence.*

Exercise

1a. **College Freshman:**

"How can I select a major here at the university? There are too many fields of study that interest me. I'm overwhelmed. I need some help in determining how to best use my college years."

Personalized Feeling (about problem): You feel _____

_____ because you _____

_____

1b. **College Freshman:**

After defining a goal: *"I didn't realize that the university career center had a sophisticated software program to help me discover the fields of study that are most aligned with my personality, interests, and abilities."*

Personalized Feeling (about goal): You feel _____

_____ because you _____

_____

2a. **Young Man:**

"I just can't stop eating! Why bother setting goals I can't control myself?"

Personalized Feeling (about problem): You feel _____

_____ because you _____

_____

2b. **Young Man:**

After defining a goal: *"I didn't think I could ever take the weight off, but now I think maybe I can."*

Personalized Feeling (about goal): You feel _____

_____ because you _____

_____

Exercise (continued)

3a. **Teenager:** *"I'd like to stop smoking pot, but it's hard to do by myself. A lot of my friends smoke. How can I say 'No!'? I just don't know if I'm willing to risk being rejected by my friends."*

    Personalized Feeling (about problem): You feel _____

_____ because you _____

_____

3b. **Teenager:** **After defining a goal:** *"I see, so if I learn to communicate to my friends that I understand them before I say 'No,' I'll show them that I respect them, and that sets them up to respect me and my decision not to smoke pot with them."*

    Personalized Feeling (about goal): You feel _____

_____ because you _____

_____

Personalizing Decision-Making

Overview

We use decision-making strategies when we want to select from among alternatives. Decision-making involves five major steps. (See pages 196–204 of *The Art of Helping* text for a detailed explanation of Decision-Making Skills.)

Step 1—Problem

We begin decision-making by describing a personalized problem. We are able to describe a problem because we have been attentive to the situation and the people involved. We have observed and listened. We have responded interchangeably to check our understanding. We have communicated our understanding of what the situation means with a personalized response to meaning. Building upon this understanding, we are now able to formulate a response that describes the personalized problem. One way to describe personal problems is to describe them as knowledge, skill, or attitude deficits.

> **Example:** *You feel directionless because you can't decide which job opportunities to pursue.*

Step 2—Goal

Next, we describe the personalized goal. One way to describe a personal goal is to describe the knowledge, skill, or attitude that would solve the problem or deficit.

> **Example:** *You feel confused because you can't decide which job opportunities to pursue and you want to be able to decide which job will be best for you.*

Step 3—Courses of Action

Now we may generate alternative courses of action. We may expand people options—"Who else might become involved?" We may expand program options—"What else might be done?" Or, we may expand organization options—"How else could we relate people and program options?"

> **Example:**
>
> - Publishing Company—Assistant Editor for a small company
> - Consulting Company—Production work on projects
> - Self-Employment—Independent sub-contractor

Step 4—Values

We select our preferred alternative by using our values. Values are the meanings we attach to people, data, and things. Values are who and what matter to us. One helpful way of describing values is to describe the living, learning, and working benefits we wish to attain. We may now list the benefits we hope to gain. (It is understood that there are no benefits without some associated costs. When we define our values or the benefits we hope to gain, we will also include information about associated costs.)

Step 4—Values (continued)

VALUES		EXAMPLE:
• Working Benefits	–	Opportunity for advancement
• Learning Benefits	–	Training opportunities
• Living Benefits	–	Finances (salary) and commute (travel time)

Step 5—Choice

Finally, we list our values and courses of action. We use our values to evaluate the courses of action. We evaluate how each course impacts each value. A helpful way of evaluating courses is to use the signs plus (+) and minus (−), or neutral (0) to represent our estimations of how well or how poorly each alternative course will satisfy each value. After making this evaluation, we calculate the best alternative.

Example:

	COURSES OF ACTION		
VALUES	Publishing Company	Consulting Company	Self-Employment
• Advancement	+	0	0
• Finances	+	+	0
• Training	+	0	−
• Commute	0	−	+

CHOICE: Assistant Editor for Publishing Company

Exercise 40: Using Decision-Making Skills

Introduction

Now you may practice these decision-making skills with a problem and goal of your own.

Instructions

Follow these five decision-making steps to determine the best solution for your problem.

Exercise

Step 1: *Define a personalized problem.*

I feel _____

because I cannot _____

Step 2: *Define a personalized goal.*

I feel _____

because I cannot _____

and I want to _____

Step 3: *Now expand your possible courses of action. (Be sure to expand people, programs, and organization of resources.)*

COURSES OF ACTION

People Alternatives	Program Alternatives	Organizational Alternatives
_____	_____	_____
_____	_____	_____
_____	_____	_____

Step 4: *List your values or the benefits you hope to gain. For example, these may be living, learning, or working benefits. (Also consider costs associated with these benefits.)*

VALUES

_____

_____

_____

_____

_____

Exercise (continued)

Step 5: *Choose which alternative best satisfies your values. Evaluate or rate your alternative courses of action by estimating how well each course will satisfy each value. Select the best choice from among your alternatives.*

For a more thorough study of decision-making, see Carkhuff, R. R. *Productive Problem-Solving.* Amherst, MA: HRD Press, 1985.

Personalizing Communication

Overview

The exercises in this chapter will provide you with opportunities to develop a series of personalized responses to helpee excerpts and to yourself.

Exercise 41: Personalizing Communication

Introduction

This exercise is designed to help you master personalizing, culminating in a personalized goal for the helpee. Along the way, you will formulate and communicate multiple interchangeable responses to meaning (externalizing responsibility) and multiple personalized responses to meaning (internalizing helpee responsibility). You may identify more than one problem before settling on a specific problem or set of problems to be transformed into a goal or goals to be accomplished.

Instructions

The statements below and on the following pages are made by two people engaged in extensive exploration: a Mother (helpee) and the Helper. After you read each statement, write your best response. Label each of your responses as an Interchangeable Response, Personalized Meaning, Personalized Problem, or Personalized Goal. (After completing each exercise, turn to the pages that follow to see how one experienced helper responded to the exercise.) To maximize your learning, do the exercise BEFORE looking at the responses made by an experienced helper.

Helpee 1: Mother

a. **Mother:** *"My children are starting to get out of hand. They've gotten so they don't listen to me or my husband unless we threaten them. And who wants to always have to threaten their children?"*

a. **Helper:** _____

_____

_____

b. **Mother:** *"It's very frustrating. The oldest boy, Jimmy, was well-behaved until this past year and then suddenly, it's like he's a different kid. He's wild now, always yelling and screaming. And last week I caught him twisting his brother's arm. I mean, he wanted to **hurt** him!"*

b. **Helper:** _____

_____

_____

Helpee 1: Mother (continued)

c. **Mother:** *"We're not a violent family. I don't know where he gets it from. Jimmy's getting mean; the kind of kid who is a bully."*

c. **Helper:** _____

_____

_____

d. **Mother:** *"It scares me. You read stories about children who do really awful things. Jimmy isn't that bad, but it could happen."*

d. **Helper:** _____

_____

_____

e. **Mother:** *"Oh, I guess I'm not that afraid. He's a good kid, actually. He can be very loving. And sometimes he's quite cooperative. It's just that I want to be sure to catch this before it's out of my control. I love my son and I don't want him growing up as some lonely bully. He should have a better life than that."*

e. **Helper:** _____

_____

_____

f. **Mother:** *"That's really it. I guess I'm sad and worried... He's always been an introverted kid. Jimmy always seems to be alone. I used to ignore it. Try to tell myself he'd get more social as he got older. He seems so shy and kinda sad when he's in a group. My husband says, 'Leave the boy alone; he'll grow out of it.' But it breaks my heart, watching him always alone. I know how much he wants to be a social person and have others welcome him."*

f. **Helper:** _____

_____

_____

g. **Mother:** *"I'm only trying to help. I don't get mad at him for having trouble making friends. If anything, I try to encourage him to get along. But, it's backfiring. The more I press, the meaner he gets."*

g. **Helper:** _____

_____

_____

Helpee 1: Mother (continued)

h.   **Mother:** *"I guess I pressure him too much sometimes, telling him what he needs to do."*

h.   **Helper:** _____

_____

_____

i.   **Mother:** *"I've never had any trouble making friends, and I've always been comfortable with people. I was never the 'star,' but I got along and I was happy."*

i.   **Helper:** _____

_____

_____

j.   **Mother:** *"I wish I could help Jimmy learn to get along with others and be happy like I was when I grew up. I know it's what he needs—to feel valued and accepted when he's with other children."*

j.   **Helper:** _____

_____

_____

k.   **Mother:** *"Jimmy's getting frustrated and I don't know what to do. I've seen this developing and I just don't seem to be handling it well. I can see that his brother has started to model after him. He's becoming a loner and showing anger too. I know that they need something from me. What can I do?"*

k.   **Helper:** _____

_____

_____

At this point in the helping session, as the helper, you would initiate to begin the action phase of the helpee learning process. You will initiate by defining action steps for the helpee to take to assist her in solving her problem; in this case, helping her to help her sons. (Initiating skills follow in the next chapter of this workbook.)

Helpee 1: Mother (continued)

Here is how one experienced helper responded to this exercise.

a. **Mother:** *"My children are starting to get out of hand. They've gotten so they don't listen to me or my husband unless we threaten them. And who wants to always have to threaten their children?"*

a. **Helper:** "You feel troubled because your children are being disrespectful to you and your husband." (**Interchangeable Response**)

b. **Mother:** *"It's very frustrating. The oldest boy, Jimmy, was well-behaved until this past year and then suddenly, it's like he's a different kid. He's wild now, always yelling and screaming. And last week I caught him twisting his brother's arm. I mean, he wanted to **hurt** him!"*

b. **Helper:** "You feel especially worried about Jimmy because his anger might result in hurting his younger brother." (**Interchangeable Response**)

c. **Mother:** *"We're not a violent family. I don't know where he gets it from. Jimmy's getting mean; the kind of kid who is a bully."*

c. **Helper:** "You feel shocked because, somehow, Jimmy has seen and adopted bullying behaviors." (**Interchangeable Response**)

d. **Mother:** *"It scares me. You read stories about children who do really awful things. Jimmy isn't that bad, but it could happen."*

d. **Helper:** "You feel afraid because Jimmy could, possibly, become more out of control." (**Interchangeable Response**)

e. **Mother:** *"Oh, I guess I'm not that afraid. He's a good kid, actually. He can be very loving. And sometimes he's quite cooperative. It's just that I want to be sure to catch this before it's out of my control. I love my son and I don't want him growing up as some lonely bully. He should have a better life than that."*

e. **Helper:** "You feel sad because you don't want Jimmy to have a difficult future." (**Personalized Meaining—Implications**)

f. **Mother:** *"That's really it. I guess I'm sad and worried… He's always been an introverted kid. Jimmy always seems to be alone. I used to ignore it. Try to tell myself he'd get more social as he got older. He seems so shy and kinda sad when he's in a group. My husband says, 'Leave the boy alone; he'll grow out of it.' But it breaks my heart, watching him always alone. I know how much he wants to be a social person and have others welcome him."*

f. **Helper:** "You feel disappointed because Jimmy hasn't yet developed the social skills he needs." (**Interchangeable Response**)

Helpee 1: Mother (continued)

g. **Mother:** *"I'm only trying to help. I don't get mad at him for having trouble making friends. If anything, I try to encourage him to get along. But, it's backfiring. The more I press, the meaner he gets."*

g. **Helper:** "You feel helpless because your encouragement antagonizes him" **(Personalized Meaning)**

h. **Mother:** *"I guess I pressure him too much sometimes, telling him what he needs to do."*

h. **Helper:** "You feel unsure of what to say or do because Jimmy is having a difficult time handling the pressure from you." **(Interchangeable Response)**

i. **Mother:** *"I've never had any trouble making friends, and I've always been comfortable with people. I was never the 'star,' but I got along and I was happy."*

i. **Helper:** "You feel puzzled because you never had to overcome the interpersonal problems that the boys are experiencing." **(Personalized Meaning)**

j. **Mother:** *"I wish I could help Jimmy learn to get along with others and be happy like I was when I grew up. I know it's what he needs—to feel valued and accepted when he's with other children."*

j. **Helper:** "You feel disappointed because you want to help Jimmy with his social skills, but you don't know how to do it." **(Personalized Problem)**

k. **Mother:** *"Jimmy's getting frustrated and I don't know what to do. I've seen this developing and I just don't seem to be handling it well. I can see that his brother has started to model after him. He's becoming a loner and showing anger too. I know that they need something from me. What can I do?"*

k. **Helper:** "You feel distressed because both boys are troubled and you don't know how to break this cycle of loneliness and anger and you want to learn how to get them the help they need." **(Personalized Problem and Personalized Goal)**

At this point in the helping session, the helper and helpee would begin the action phase of the helpee learning process. The helper will initiate by defining action steps for the helpee to take to assist her in solving her problem; in this case, helping her help her sons.

Helpee 2: Ex-Convict

a. **Ex-Con:**   *"I've been looking hard, but they don't give you a fair break. Once they know you've got that prison record, they judge the record, not the man. They leave no room for people who have changed."*

a. **Helper:**   _____

_____

_____

b. **Ex-Con:**   *"I feel trapped! Sure, I made mistakes when I was younger. What I did was wrong. But if I can't get a job, I'll have no choice. If I have to rob to feed myself, I'll rob!"*

b. **Helper:**   _____

_____

_____

c. **Ex-Con:**   *"Employers see my record and look at me like they're afraid of me when I apply for jobs. They don't want me."*

c. **Helper:**   _____

_____

_____

d. **Ex-Con:**   *"When I was in prison, I went through a career training program learning business and computer networking skills. And years ago, I did some work as a salesman. I was good at it too. What difference does it make though? With my clothes, I even look like an ex-con! After five minutes of side looks from those interviewers, I start to feel and act like what they think of me."*

d. **Helper:**   _____

_____

_____

e. **Ex-Con:**   *"There's just no room for me in that world out there."*

e. **Helper:**   _____

_____

_____

Helpee 2: Ex-Convict (continued)

f. **Ex-Con:** *"I'd be a good employee. I've got a lot to prove...to others...and to myself. It's time I get a chance to handle the world. I know I'd work hard and do what they asked, as best as I could...If I could just get that first job."*

f. **Helper:** _____

_____

_____

g. **Ex-Con:** *"But I always blow the interview. They start to question me about my record and I react with a deep breath and a quiet moment. I start thinkin', 'Here we go again!' I know that makes them suspicious, too. If I can't talk about it, I must still be a criminal."*

g. **Helper:** _____

_____

_____

h. **Ex-Con:** *"If I could learn how to handle them when they come at me about my record, that might help."*

h. **Helper:** _____

_____

_____

i. **Ex-Con:** *"I always feel so bad by the time I finish a job interview. I've been a loser for too long."*

i. **Helper:** _____

_____

_____

j. **Ex-Con:** *"Yeah, I guess I'm vulnerable to the way they think. I start to feel like I'm being judged and I just sink right into it. I don't project myself; I just act the way I think they're seeing me. I never seem to keep showing my positive side. I give up."*

j. **Helper:** _____

_____

_____

Helpee 2: Ex-Convict (continued)

k. **Ex-Con:** *"Yeah, I want to communicate that I've got skills to offer and tell them who I am. I want to communicate that I'm a 'can-do guy," I'm willing to learn and work with others, and I have determination to be successful! Can you help me communicate that?"*

k. **Helper:** _____

_____

_____

l. **Ex-Con:** *"Okay, let's do it!"*

At this point in the helping session, as the helper, you would initiate to begin the action phase of the helpee learning process. You will initiate by defining action steps for the helpee to take to assist him in solving his problem; in this case, helping him to improve his job interviewing skills.

Helpee 2: Ex-Convict (continued)

Here is how one experienced helper responded to this exercise.

a. **Ex-Con:** *"I've been looking hard, but they don't give you a fair break. Once they know you've got that prison record, they judge the record, not the man. They leave no room for people who have changed."*

a. **Helper:** "You feel angry because people judge you by your past and not who you are today." **(Interchangeable Response)**

b. **Ex-Con:** *"I feel trapped! Sure, I made mistakes when I was younger. What I did was wrong. But if I can't get a job, I'll have no choice. If I have to rob to feed myself, I'll rob!"*

b. **Helper:** "You feel trapped because no one will give you a job and a chance to be free of the trap." **(Interchangeable Response)**

c. **Ex-Con:** *"Employers see my record and look at me like they're afraid of me when I apply for jobs. They don't want me."*

c. **Helper:** "You feel hated because they see the old you and disregard the person in front of them." **(Interchangeable Response)**

d. **Ex-Con:** *"When I was in prison, I went through a career training program learning business and computer networking skills. And years ago, I did some work as a salesman. I was good at it too. What difference does it make though? With my clothes, I even look like an ex-con! After five minutes of side looks from those interviewers, I start to feel and act like what they think of me."*

d. **Helper:** "You feel frustrated because despite your valuable career skills, you still don't get considered for the job." **(Personalized Meaning)**

e. **Ex-Con:** *"There's just no room for me in that world out there."*

e. **Helper:** "You feel rejected because no one has let you in; given you a chance." **(Interchangeable Response)**

f. **Ex-Con:** *"I'd be a good employee. I've got a lot to prove...to others...and to myself. It's time I get a chance to handle the world. I know I'd work hard and do what they asked, as best as I could...If I could just get that first job."*

f. **Helper:** "You feel confident in yourself because you've got some valuable skills and an *'I will succeed'* attitude." **(Personalized Meaning)**

Helpee 2: Ex-Convict (continued)

g. **Ex-Con:** *"But I always blow the interview. They start to question me about my record and I react with a deep breath and a quiet moment. I start thinkin', 'Here we go again!' I know that makes them suspicious, too. If I can't talk about it, I must still be a criminal."*

g. **Helper:** "You feel disappointed because you automatically react to questions about your criminal record with the thought of being denied a job opportunity once again." **(Personalized Meaning)**

h. **Ex-Con:** *"If I could learn how to handle them when they come at me about my record, that might help."*

h. **Helper:** "You feel held back because you haven't reacted well to questions about your record and you want to be able to react better." **(Personalized Problem and Personalized Goal)**

i. **Ex-Con:** *"I always feel so bad by the time I finish a job interview. I've been a loser for too long."*

i. **Helper:** "You feel discouraged because, so far, you've been unable to get that first job and restart your life." **(Personalized Meaning)**

j. **Ex-Con:** *"Yeah, I guess I'm vulnerable to the way they think. I start to feel like I'm being judged and I just sink right into it. I don't project myself; I just act the way I think they're seeing me. I never seem to keep showing my positive side. I give up."*

j. **Helper:** "You feel upset with yourself because you let the prejudices of the interviewers stop you from telling them about the confident and skilled man that you are, and you want to be able to present that man to potential employers." **(Personalized Problem and Personalized Goal)**

k. **Ex-Con:** *"Yeah, I want to communicate that I've got skills to offer and tell them who I am. I want to communicate that I'm a 'can-do guy,' I'm willing to learn and work with others, and I have determination to be successful! Can you help me communicate that?"*

k. **Helper:** "I will be happy to work with you to improve your interviewing skills! You feel reinvigorated… and dedicated to learning better interviewing skills because you see winning a job and having a job as a way to finally live as a free man." **(Personalized Changed Feelings and Personalized Meaning)**

l. **Ex-Con:** *"Okay, let's do it!"*

At this point in the helping session, the helper and helpee would begin the action phase of the helpee learning process, helping him to improve his job interviewing skills.

Exercise 42: Personalizing with Yourself

Introduction

You can use your personalizing skills to help understand your own problems too. In the following exercises, you will help yourself to take control of your experience.

Instructions

Follow the instructions within each of the sections, then write responses to yourself.

Exercise 1

a. Go back to Exercise 30 on page 72 in this workbook and use one of the statements you wrote or select a different situation or experience that is important to you. Describe that situation here.

_____

_____

_____

_____

_____

b. Write an interchangeable response to yourself. (Be sure to take time to explore how you feel about the experience and why you feel this way.)

I feel _____ because _____

_____

c. Think about (explore) the situation further and write three more interchangeable responses to yourself.

I feel _____ because _____

_____

I feel _____ because _____

_____

I feel _____ because _____

_____

Exercise 1 (concluded)

d. Write a personalized meaning response to yourself for the same situation. (You may decide to personalize responsibility for your experience, personalize the implications or consequences of your behaviors, or personalize your assumptions or beliefs.)

I feel _____ because I _____

_____

_____

e. Write another personalized meaning response to yourself for the same situation.

I feel _____ because I _____

_____

_____

f. Write a personalized problem response to yourself for the same situation. (Try to be specific about identifying a deficit in your knowledge or skills, or a bad attitude that is contributing to the situation.)

I feel _____ because I cannot _____

_____

_____

g. Write a personalized goal response to yourself for the same situation. (An effective goal is the "flipside" of a problem. It is the asset you need as a replacement for your current deficit.)

I feel _____ because I cannot _____

_____

_____

and I want to _____

_____

_____

Exercise 2

a. Briefly describe another situation or experience which is important to you.

_____

_____

_____

_____

_____

b. Write a series of six interchangeable responses to yourself. After you write each response, be sure to take time to explore how you feel about the experience and why. Expand your exploration by using different feeling words and reasons for these feelings.

I feel _____ because _____

_____

_____

I feel _____ because _____

_____

_____

I feel _____ because _____

_____

_____

I feel _____ because _____

_____

_____

I feel _____ because _____

_____

_____

I feel _____ because _____

_____

_____

Exercise 2 (continued)

c. Write a personalized meaning response to yourself. (You may decide to personalize responsibility for your experience; personalize the implications or consequences of your behaviors; or personalize your assumptions or beliefs.)

I feel _____ because I _____

_____

_____

d. Write another personalized meaning response to yourself.

I feel _____ because I _____

_____

_____

e. Write a personalized problem response to yourself. (Try to be specific about identifying a deficit in your knowledge or skills or a bad attitude that is contributing to the situation.)

I feel _____ because I cannot _____

_____

_____

f. Write a personalized goal response to yourself. (An effective goal is the "flipside" of a problem. It is the asset you need as a replacement for your current deficit.)

I feel _____ because I cannot _____

_____

_____

and I want to _____

_____

_____

❺ Initiating: Facilitating Helpee Acting

Overview

As a helper, you have attended to involve your helpees. You responded with accuracy to assist them to explore their experiences. You co-processed to develop personalized, individualized responses to help them expand the depth of their understanding of the meaning of their situations and helped them identify their problems and goals. Finally, the helpees have reached the acting phase. The helper skills of initiating will support the helpees to solve their problems and reach their goals.

Initiating skills involve defining the goal, developing the steps to the goal, determining a schedule for completing the steps and for reinforcing the achievement of the goal. An example of initiating is given below, followed by exercises.

Before you complete the exercises in this chapter, read pages 215–255 in *The Art of Helping* text.

Example:

Personalized Goal:

You feel helpless inside because you cannot communicate in a helpful way with your children and you want to communicate effectively with them.

Operationalized Goal:

You want to communicate effectively with your children by building an interchangeable base of communication, as indicated by the number of interchangeable responses you make to them at home.

Steps to the Goal:

1. Arrange room to attend contextually

   a. Arrange furniture without barriers
   b. Eliminate distractions

2. Attend posturally

   a. Square
   b. Lean
   c. Make eye contact

3. Respond to content

   a. Listen to 5WH (who, what, when, where, why, and how)
   b. Recall
   c. Communicate: "You're saying _____."

Example (continued)

4. Respond to feeling
    a. Ask yourself, "How would I feel if I were that person?"
    b. Select category and intensity
    c. Communicate: "You feel _____."

5. Respond to meaning
    a. Recall main theme
    b. Identify feeling and reason for the feeling
    c. Communicate: "You feel _____ because _____."

Schedule for learning these communication skills through a 5-week program:

STEPS	START	FINISH
1. Attend Contextually	February 8	February 8
2. Attend Posturally	February 8	February 8
3. Respond to Content	February 8	Continue through program
4. Respond to Feeling	February 15	Continue through program
5. Respond to Meaning (Feeling and Content)	February 22	Continue through program: check: 2/29, 3/7, 3/14

Reinforcements:

Positive: *Dinner at a restaurant with the family or take-out food (dinner with family at home).*

Negative: Complete a housework project you've been putting off.

Exercise 43: Exploring Initiating Skills

Introduction

This exercise will help you understand your personal experiences with initiating.

Instructions

Answer each of the questions in the exercise below.

Exercise

1. Describe a goal that *you* have successfully achieved.

   _____

   _____

   _____

   _____

   _____

2. Why do you think you were able to reach your goal? What did *you* do that made it possible?

   _____

   _____

   _____

   _____

   _____

3. Describe a goal that *you* failed to achieve.

   _____

   _____

   _____

   _____

   _____

4. Why did *you* fail? What is it that *you* did or *you* did not do that resulted in your failure?

   _____

   _____

   _____

   _____

   _____

Exercise 44: Practicing Defining Goals

Introduction

This exercise will help you learn to write operational goals. An operational goal specifies the intended **behavior** and specifies a **standard** (a way to measure performance).

In defining the goal, we need to establish all of the ingredients necessary to achieve the goal. We accomplish this by specifying the "5WH information" (who, what, when, where, why, and how) about the goal and by specifying a standard (how well) to measure performance: "How will we know when we have reached our goal?"

- **Who** or **what** is involved in the goal?
- **What** will the people and/or things involved do?
- **How** and **why** will it be done?
- **Where** and **when** will it be done?
- **Where** and **when** will it be done?
- **How well** will it be done?

Next, we must communicate our definition of the goal to the helpee in these operational terms. We do this by emphasizing observable and measurable behaviors and standards of performance. Standards are usually described in terms of the number of times or the amount of time the helpee will perform some behavior.

Instructions

For each of the following situations, make the goal operational by answering the interrogatives. After you answer the interrogatives, write a statement that communicates this goal to the helpee, stating what will be done (behavior) and how well it will be done (standards of performance).

Example:

A teenage girl feels estranged from her father, who has just rejoined the family after living and working away in a foreign country for several years.

a. **Personalized goal:**

You feel disappointed because you can't relate effectively to your father and you want to be able to.

b. **Operationalized goal:**

Who or What:	*helpee and father*
What:	*to relate effectively*
How and Why:	*by responding accurately to increase communication*
When and Where:	*at home during meal times*
How Well:	*lay an interchangeable base—at least three responses*

Example (continued)

c. **Communicate the goal to the helpee:**

*You want to relate effectively by building an interchangeable base of communications with your parents **(behavior)** as indicated by three interchangeable responses you make to your father at home during meal times **(standards).***

Exercise

1. A freshman girl (from a very small town) is now at a large college and refuses to leave her roommate's side.

   a. **Personalized goal:**

   You feel lost because you don't know how to go about making new friends and you want to learn how to.

   b. **Operationalized goal:**

   Who or What: _____

   What: _____

   How and Why: _____

   When and Where: _____

   How Well: _____

   c. **Communicate the goal to the helpee:**

   You want to _____

   _____

   _____ **(BEHAVIOR)**

   As indicated by _____

   _____

   _____ **(STANDARDS)**

2. A man in his early 30s has been complaining about his wife always nagging him, yet he very frequently is the one to initiate the arguments.

   a. **Personalized goal:**

   You feel disappointed because you can't control your temper with your wife and you desperately want to prevent arguments.

Exercise 2 (continued)

b. Operationalized goal:

Who or What: _____

What: _____

How and Why: _____

When and Where: _____

How Well: _____

c. Communicate the goal to the helpee:

You want to _____

_____

_____ **(BEHAVIOR)**

As indicated by _____

_____

_____ **(STANDARDS)**

3. A businesswoman is passed over for a position as manager of a department.

a. Personalized goal:

You feel trapped because you can't describe demonstrable, clear evidence of your managerial ability and you want to be able to prove your ability.

b. Operationalized goal:

Who or What: _____

What: _____

How and Why: _____

When and Where: _____

How Well: _____

c. Communicate the goal to the helpee:

You want to _____

_____

_____ **(BEHAVIOR)**

As indicated by _____

_____

_____ **(STANDARDS)**

Exercise (continued)

4. A young, first-time offender continues to be harassed by one particular prison guard who likes to threaten him.

   a. **Personalized goal:**

   You feel scared because you can't handle the guard's threats and you want to be able to.

   b. **Operationalized goal:**

   Who or What: _____

   What: _____

   How and Why: _____

   When and Where: _____

   How Well: _____

   c. **Communicate the goal to the helpee:**

   You want to _____

   _____ **(BEHAVIOR)**

   As indicated by _____

   _____ **(STANDARDS)**

5. An elderly man is talking about his realization that as time is running out, he wants to leave a legacy by writing his life story. He says that he owes it to his family, friends, and others to write about his most interesting and meaningful life stories. He says that he won't allow himself to procrastinate any longer.

   a. **Personalized goal:**

   You feel disappointed that you haven't yet documented your life story and you're committed to writing about it.

   b. **Operationalized goal:**

   Who or What: _____

   What: _____

   How and Why: _____

   When and Where: _____

   How Well: _____

Exercise (continued)

c. **Communicate the goal to the helpee:**

You want to _____

_____

_____ **(BEHAVIOR)**

As indicated by _____

_____

_____ **(STANDARDS)**

Developing Programs

Overview

Initiating steps to the goal means identifying and sequencing the first step, the intermediate steps, and the necessary sub-steps that the person must do in order to reach the goal.

Before completing these exercises, review the section on Developing Programs in *The Art of Helping* text on pages 224–244.

Exercise 45: Making Sure the Steps to a Goal are Behaviors

Introduction

Steps to the goal should be observable and measurable behaviors. A good step is specific and tells the person what he or she will do.

Instructions

Identify which of the steps below are observable and measurable behaviors. Check **yes** if the step is a behavior, and **no** if it is not a behavior.

Example:

	BEHAVIOR	
	YES	NO
1. Try harder	☐	☑
2. Read one book	☑	☐
3. Attend posturally	☑	☐
4. Get in shape	☐	☑
5. Run a half mile	☑	☐
6. Be more open	☐	☑

Exercise

BEHAVIOR

	YES	NO
1. Rewrite the essay	☐	☐
2. Ask two questions	☐	☐
3. Be curious	☐	☐
4. Act creative	☐	☐
5. Think fast	☐	☐
6. Recall 5WH interrogative information	☐	☐
7. Make a personalized response to meaning	☐	☐
8. Do 15 sit-ups	☐	☐
9. Track caloric intake per day	☐	☐
10. Eat less	☐	☐
11. Lose weight	☐	☐
12. Sit down for dinner without any electronic device	☐	☐
13. Be empathic	☐	☐
14. Call your parents once a week	☐	☐
15. Feel more confident	☐	☐
16. Watch less television	☐	☐
17. Ignore it	☐	☐
18. Submit your resume to an online job site	☐	☐
19. Plan ahead	☐	☐
20. Confront her	☐	☐
21. List two assets	☐	☐
22. Relax	☐	☐
23. Make a verbal response to her feelings	☐	☐
24. Don't get depressed	☐	☐
25. Spend a half-hour alone	☐	☐

(Exercise 45 answers are on page 182.)

Exercise 46: Practicing Developing Steps

Introduction

To develop steps to a goal, begin by brainstorming a list of the behaviors necessary for a person to accomplish his or her goal.

Instructions

For each of the following people, brainstorm possible steps (behaviors) to lead them to accomplish their operationalized goal. You do not need to develop a step for each available line provided; however, in this exercise, identify at least 5 steps for each goal. Remember that steps are "behaviors."

Example:

Janine: Janine is a 24-year-old mother of two. Ashley is 2½ years of age and is walking and climbing everywhere. Allison, the baby, is almost 14 months old. She's up on her feet too and getting more mobile each day. They are happy babies with one exception: they both have terrible skin rashes and the rashes affect them emotionally. When their skin conditions are very dry and blotchy looking, they get very irritable. What is Janine to do?

Janine's first operationalized goal:

"I want to try some health initiatives that will minimize the severity of the children's rashes as indicated by a reduction in dry, blotchy skin and by a reduction in irritable behaviors exhibited by the children."

Brainstorm some steps for Janine:

Keep a diary of what the children eat

Vacuum the rugs at the end of each day

Keep the dog out of the rooms where the children sleep

Invest in a quality air cleaner

Take the children to the doctor for a checkup

Get dust mite covers for the children's mattresses

Exercise

1. **Sam:** Sam is an 18-year-old drug user—he smokes marijuana, drinks alcohol, takes pills, and snorts cocaine. Sam came in complaining of feeling alone, abused, and disgusted with himself. He is in poor physical shape, standing 5'11" and weighing only 137 pounds. Sam graduated from high school last year with no vocational skills and only a C- average. He has few friends and considers the friends he has to be a negative influence. Sam is depressed and scared about his future.

Sam's first operationalized goal:

"I want to quit smoking pot, drinking, and taking other drugs as indicated by the number of days I am 'clean' (without drugs or alcohol)."

Brainstorm some steps for Sam:

Exercise (continued)

2. **Rita:** Rita is suffering from a severe bout with depression. She was a relatively happy person until 3 months ago when she caught her husband in bed with another woman. She has left her husband and is staying with her sister and her sister's husband. Rita finds that the littlest reminder of her estranged husband sets her off into fits of crying. She is both furious at him and full of pain. Rita has filed for divorce. She is feeling down because at age 40, she is without a life partner or a full-time job. She is terrified that she will end up spending the rest of her life in poverty and alone.

Rita's first operationalized goal:

"I want to regain my self-worth and dignity as indicated by the number of days of work that I can get this month."

Brainstorm some steps for Rita:

Exercise (continued)

3. **Mary:** Mary is a 35-year-old who has a phobia of crowds. Whenever she goes to a public place and crowds begin to form near her, she begins to feel trapped. She starts to feel panicky. Her jaw begins to tighten, and her breathing becomes shallow and speeds up. When Mary starts feeling this way, she quickly makes her way to an exit to escape the crowd. Recently, Mary went shopping at her local mall. She entered a store and did some shopping, but when she exited the store, she found that the mall was filling with people and she started to feel panicked. Mary does not want this fear to keep her from living a normal life.

Mary's first operationalized goal:

"I want to be able to walk among a crowd of people as indicated by the length of time I can go to a busy, crowded mall and not feel overwhelmed and feel forced to escape."

Brainstorm some steps for Mary:

Exercise 47: Practicing Developing Sub-Steps

Introduction

This exercise will increase your ability to divide a behavior into smaller behaviors or sub-steps. Sub-steps increase the likelihood that the person will achieve a goal. Sub-steps should be observable and measurable behaviors that lead to a step in a program. Develop sub-steps by first brainstorming the behaviors necessary to accomplish a step and then sequence these behaviors as sub-steps.

Instructions

On the following pages, use the steps that you brainstormed in Exercise 46, then develop appropriate sub-steps for each step. Use only as many steps and sub-steps as you feel are necessary. Ignore the Start and Finish dates for now. They will be addressed in the next exercise.

Example:

Operationalized Goal:

I want to get in shape as indicated by the number of miles I run each week.

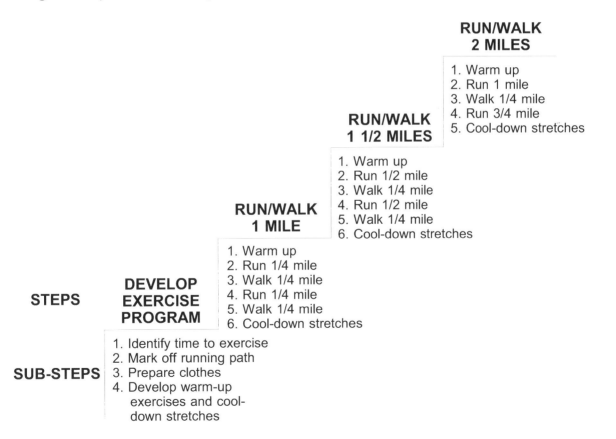

Note: The step ladder form used above and on the following pages is one way to represent an entire program. If you prefer, you may also write your program in the more familiar outline form, as shown on the following page.

Example (continued)

Operationalized Goal:

I want to get in shape as indicated by the number of miles I run each week.

I. Develop Exercise Program
1. Identify time to exercise
2. Mark off running path
3. Prepare clothes
4. Develop warm-up exercises and cool-down stretches

II. Run/Walk 1 Mile
1. Warm up
2. Run ¼ mile
3. Walk ¼ mile
4. Run ¼ mile
5. Walk ¼ mile
6. Cool-down stretches

III. Run/Walk 1½ Miles
1. Warm up
2. Run ½ mile
3. Walk ¼ mile
4. Run ½ mile
5. Walk ¼ mile
6. Cool-down stretches

IV. Run/Walk 2 Miles
1. Warm up
2. Run 1 mile
3. Walk ¼ mile
4. Run ¾ mile
5. Cool-down stretches

Exercise

1. **Sam:** "I want to quit smoking pot, drinking, and taking other drugs as indicated by the number of days I am 'clean' (without alcohol or drugs) this month."

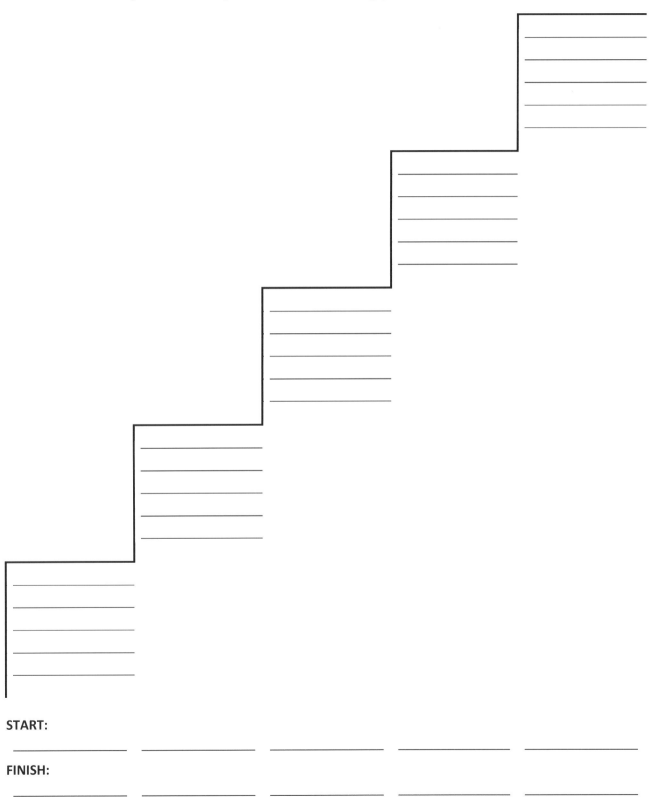

START:

_____ _____ _____ _____ _____

FINISH:

_____ _____ _____ _____ _____

Exercise (continued)

2. **Rita:** "I want to quit smoking pot, drinking, and taking other drugs as indicated by the number of days I am 'clean' (without alcohol or drugs) this month."

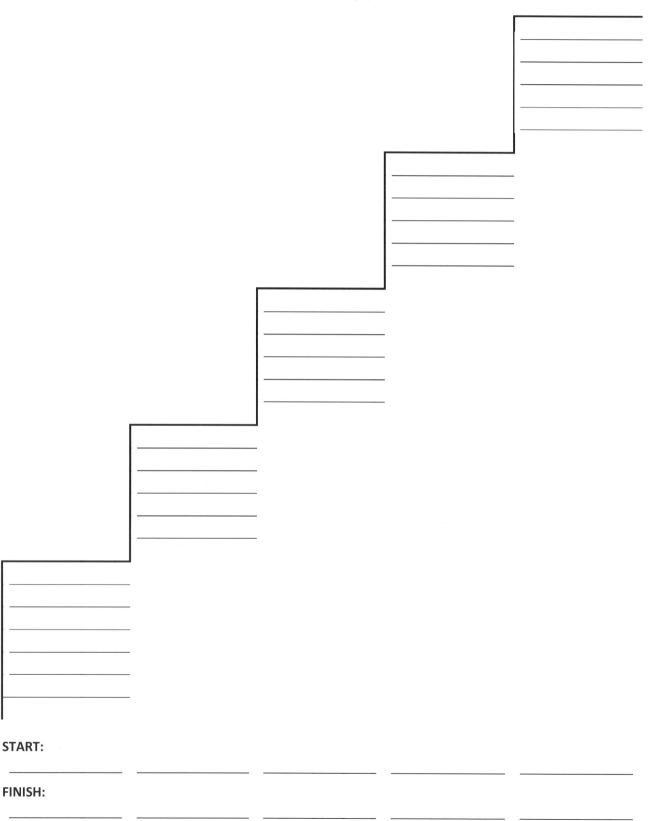

START:

_____ _____ _____ _____ _____

FINISH:

_____ _____ _____ _____ _____

Exercise (continued)

3. **Mary:** "I want to be able to walk among a crowd of people as indicated by the length of time I can go to a busy, crowded mall and not feel overwhelmed and feel forced to escape."

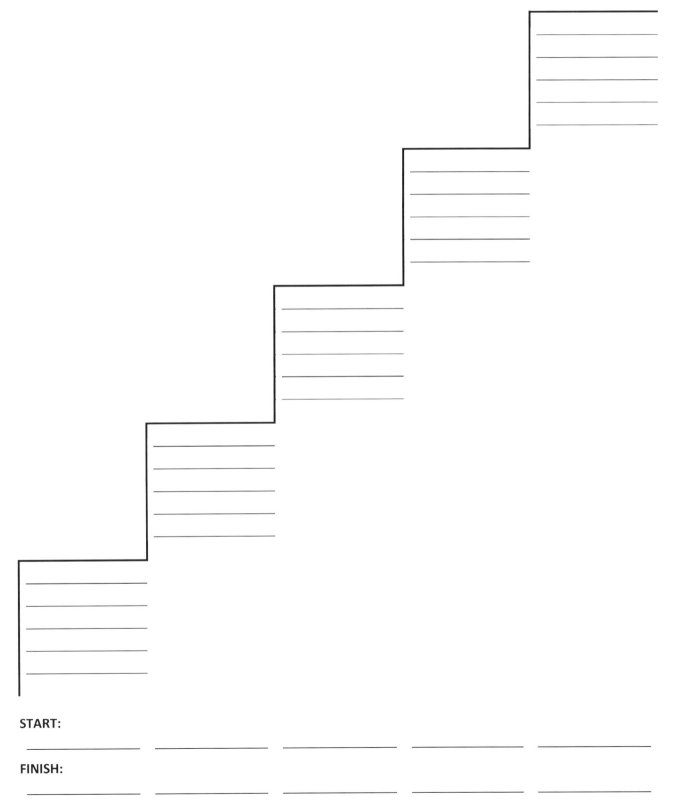

START:

_____ _____ _____ _____ _____

FINISH:

_____ _____ _____ _____ _____

Developing Schedules

Overview

Scheduling means setting a starting date and a finishing date for each step (not necessarily for each sub-step) that the person must take to achieve the goal.

Review pages 229–232 on Developing Schedules in *The Art of Helping* text before completing this section.

Exercise 48: Practicing Developing Schedules

Instructions

Go back to the steps you chose for Exercise 47 and write start and finish dates for each step in two of the three programs. Use the lines provided at the bottom of each of those pages. Imagine that the helpees (Sam, Rita, Mary) are starting their programs tomorrow.

Developing Reinforcements

Overview

Developing reinforcements encourages the helpee to take the needed steps by defining specific consequences for his/her actions.

Review pages 233–236 on Developing Reinforcements in *The Art of Helping* text before completing this section.

Exercise 49: Discriminating Types of Reinforcements

Introduction

This exercise will help you expand the repertoire of reinforcers you might use with any helpee.

When initiating a program, you can use two types of reinforcers:

➢ **Positive Reinforcers:** Adding a *desirable* consequence for completing a step in the program.

➢ **Negative Reinforcers:** Withholding something *desirable* or adding something *disliked* as a consequence for *not* completing a step in the program.

Instructions

Indicate whether each item is a positive or negative reinforcer.

Example:

	POSITIVE	NEGATIVE
1. Movie tickets for two	☑	☐
2. Not being able to use the family car	☐	☑
3. Not allowed to participate in my team's next game	☐	☑
4. Not having to mow the lawn	☑	☐

Exercise

		POSITIVE	NEGATIVE
1.	a. Buy new earphones	☐	☐
	b. Not getting to view or use social media after dinner	☐	☐
	c. Having to vacuum all the carpets in the house	☐	☐
	d. Permission to invite three friends to an overnight videogames event	☐	☐
2.	a. Being grounded (must stay home)	☐	☐
	b. Having to clean the bathroom	☐	☐
	c. Getting to stay out one hour later than usual	☐	☐
	d. Not going to a movie with friends	☐	☐
3.	a. Earning an "A" on a paper	☐	☐
	b. One "skip a homework assignment pass"	☐	☐
	c. Getting permission to go on a field trip	☐	☐
	d. Completing an extra written assignment if paper is late	☐	☐
4.	a. Two hours of yard work	☐	☐
	b. An opportunity to be the starting pitcher for the baseball team	☐	☐
	c. Offered to perform a solo in the school musical	☐	☐
	d. Two-month subscription to a mobile phone music service	☐	☐
5.	a. Getting a hot fudge sundae	☐	☐
	b. Not getting a hot fudge sundae	☐	☐
	c. Twenty dollars	☐	☐
	d. Public acknowledgement for a job well done	☐	☐

(Exercise 49 answers are on page 183.)

Exercise 50: Practicing Developing Reinforcements

Introduction

This exercise will help you to expand the reinforcements you employ for yourself and others.

Instructions

Develop a positive reinforcement and negative reinforcement for each of the three people you wrote a program for in Exercise 47 (Sam, Rita, Mary). Remember to keep the reinforcements appropriate for the goal and to make them fit the person's frame of reference.

Example:

1. **William:** *"I want to improve how our home looks as indicated by repainting the dining room and living room before the end of the month."*

    a. **Positive Reinforcement:** Overnight hotel stay at the beach with my wife

    b. **Negative Reinforcement:** $50 donation to a charity of my wife's choosing for every 7 days late in project completion

Exercise

1. **Sam:** *"I want to quit smoking pot, drinking, and taking other drugs as indicated by the number of days I am 'clean' (without drugs or alcohol) this month."*

    a. **Positive Reinforcement:** _____

    b. **Negative Reinforcement:** _____

2. **Rita:** *"I want to regain my self-worth and dignity as indicated by the number of days of work that I can get this month."*

    a. **Positive Reinforcement:** _____

    b. **Negative Reinforcement:** _____

3. **Mary:** *"I want to be able to walk among a crowd of people as indicated by the length of time I can go to a busy, crowded mall and not feel overwhelmed and feel forced to escape."*

    a. **Positive Reinforcement:** _____

    b. **Negative Reinforcement:** _____

Implementing Steps

Overview

You and your helpee will initiate to prepare your helpee for action. Together, operationalize the goal. Define the goal as *behaviors* with *standards* to measure successful performance. Then, develop steps and sub-steps, schedules/ timelines, and reinforcements.

Exercise 51: Practicing Initiating

Introduction

This exercise will help you rehearse all of the steps of initiating.

Instructions

Daniel has come to you for help. You have attended to him, responded to his exploration, and personalized his goal. Now you must initiate to help him act. In initiating with Daniel, you will operationalize his goal, develop steps to the goal, sub-steps for each step, and initiate a schedule and reinforcements.

Example:

Review examples from Exercises 43 through 50 as needed.

Exercise

Background: Daniel is 13 years old. He is a head taller than almost all of his peers and feels awkward. He is quiet and shy. Although he does not earn high grades in school, he does his school work and does not get into any trouble. Daniel usually goes unnoticed, but on one occasion, a teacher saw that he had written the words, "alone," "I'm nobody," "worthless," and had made drawings of knives on a piece of paper. Daniel had crumbled up the paper and tossed it in the classroom trash can before going to lunch. The teacher recovered the paper for a closer look, took a picture of it with her phone, and sent it to his school counselor, suggesting that the counselor meet with Daniel.

During the counseling interview, Daniel revealed that he was lonely and had no real friends. He felt trapped in a shell of shyness and didn't see any way to break out of it. Nobody showed much interest in him and Daniel felt lonely, isolated, and depressed.

Exercise (continued)

1. Write a personalized goal for Daniel:

    You feel _____

    because you cannot _____

    _____

    and you want to _____

    _____

2. Operationalize Daniel's goal (5WH Behavior and Standards).

    You want to _____

    _____

    as indicated by _____

    _____

3. Initiate steps to Daniel's operationalized goal.

Brainstorm Steps	Sequence

Exercise (concluded)

4. List steps and sub-steps:

(staircase diagram with blank lines for steps and sub-steps)

START:

_____ _____ _____ _____ _____

FINISH:

_____ _____ _____ _____ _____

5. Initiate a schedule for Daniel. Enter start and finish dates. Assume that Daniel will begin his program today.

6. List reinforcements for Daniel.

    a. **Positive Reinforcement(s):** _____

    _____

    b. **Negative Reinforcement(s):** _____

    _____

Exercise 52: Initiating with Yourself

Introduction

You are ready to initiate with your own experience using the steps you learned for initiating with others. Turn back to Exercise 42 and review the base of interchangeable responses and personalized responses you wrote to yourself.

Instructions

Write personalized responses and a program for yourself including goals, steps, schedule, and reinforcements. Follow the directions given at each point.

Exercise

1. Review your personalized goal:

    I feel _____

    because I cannot _____

    and I want to _____

2. Operationalize your goal:

    I want to _____

    as indicated by _____

    _____

3. Initiate steps to your operationalized goal.

Brainstorm Steps	Sequence

Exercise (continued)

4. List steps and sub-steps:

START:

—————————   —————————   —————————   —————————   —————————

FINISH:

—————————   —————————   —————————   —————————   —————————

5. Initiate a schedule for yourself. Enter start and finish dates. Assume that you will begin your program today.

6. List reinforcements for yourself.

    a. **Positive Reinforcement(s):** _____

    _____

    b. **Negative Reinforcement(s):** _____

    _____

Exercise 53: Reviewing Program Steps

Introduction

Implementation steps enable us to implement our programs. They include reviewing, rehearsing, and revising steps.

Reviewing is the first implementation step and involves reviewing all of the steps in the program. It gives us a chance to make sure that we have included all the necessary steps.

Instructions

Refer back to your program in the previous exercise, Exercise 52, of this workbook. Review the definition of your goal, steps of your program, time schedule, and reinforcements. Indicate any changes that you make in the space provided.

Your review:

_____

_____

_____

_____

_____

_____

_____

_____

Exercise 54: Rehearsing Program Steps

Introduction

This exercise will help you practice the next step of program implementation—rehearsing the steps. Rehearsing involves having your helpee practice a skill in a controlled setting before attempting the program steps in the intended setting. Rehearsal increases the probability of achieving the goal.

Instructions

Read the following situations and indicate how the helpees could rehearse their skills before attempting their actual goals.

Example:

A young man defines his goal as wanting to communicate effectively with his wife, as indicated by responding verbally to her feelings and the content she expresses.

He could rehearse the steps to his goal by: *practicing his responding skills within a*

classroom or helping setting to ensure mastering the skills before attempting his goal.

Exercise

1. A young woman wants to be honest with her boyfriend as indicated by the number of times she tells him her true feelings.

    She could rehearse the steps to her goal by: _____

    _____

    _____

    _____

    _____

2. A factory worker wants a higher salary as indicated by his ability to ask his boss for a raise.

    He could rehearse the steps to his goal by: _____

    _____

    _____

    _____

    _____

Exercise (continued)

3. An alcoholic wants to face her drinking problem as indicated by her ability to state to her family that she is an alcoholic.

   She could rehearse the steps to her goal by: _____

   _____

   _____

   _____

   _____

4. A budding musician wants to share three songs that she wrote as indicated by playing her guitar and singing the songs for some elderly family friends.

   She could rehearse the steps to her goal by: _____

   _____

   _____

   _____

   _____

5. A middle-aged man wants to reach out to an estranged relative as measured by sending some old pictures and a short letter, followed by initiating with a phone conversation and an invitation to get together in person.

   He could rehearse the steps to his goal by: _____

   _____

   _____

   _____

   _____

Exercise 55: Revising Program Steps or Goals

Introduction

Revising is the third implementation step. When we act on our programs, we get feedback which will indicate if we need to revise any steps or goals in our programs.

Instructions

Read the following helpee situations and revise the programs based on the feedback given.

Example:

A woman's goal is to run 3 miles in 25 minutes within 6 weeks. In the fourth week of her program, she realizes the goal is unrealistic.

A possible revision could be: *instead of running 3 miles in 25 minutes, she will revise the time to 30 minutes.*

Exercise

1. A college student's goal is to read one new novel a week, but he realizes that he does not have enough time to do this.

    A possible revision could be: _____

    _____

    _____

2. A young executive has begun managing three projects, but learns that his skills in management are poor. He does not want the projects to fail.

    A possible revision could be: _____

    _____

    _____

3. A doctor puts his patient on a 1,000-calorie-per-day diet. After one week of this, feedback indicates that his patient cannot stick to this diet because the patient does not know how to count calories.

    A possible revision could be: _____

    _____

    _____

Planning Check Steps

Overview

We can build success into our programs by developing before, during, and after check steps. Check steps emphasize the physical, emotional, and intellectual resources we need to complete each step. Review pages 241–244 in *The Art of Helping* text for more information on Planning Check Steps.

Exercise 56: Planning Check Steps

Introduction

This exercise will enable you to develop detailed programs so that you ensure the success of your goals. Check steps emphasize the things we need to think about before, during, and after the performance of each step.

> **Before Check Steps** ask and answer the question: "What resources will I need to be able to perform the step successfully?"

> **During Check Steps** ask and answer the question: "Am I performing the step correctly?"

> **After Check Steps** ask and answer the question: "Did I achieve the results and get the benefits I wanted?"

Instructions

Read the following programs. As an exercise, for each of the steps, generate an appropriate before, during, and after check step question.

Example:

A 40-year-old woman states her goal:

"I want to get in shape as indicated by the number of miles I run each week."

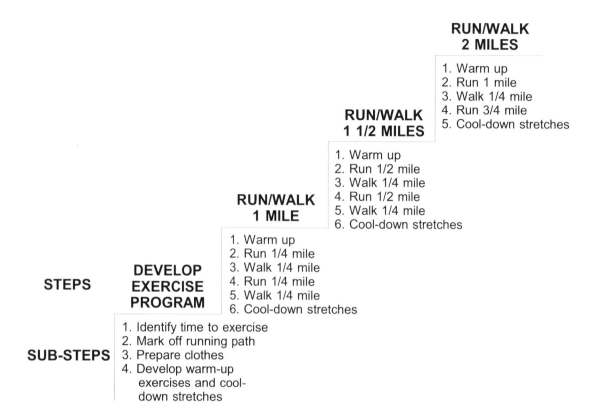

BEFORE:	BEFORE:	BEFORE:	BEFORE:
Do I have the distance measured? Do I have a stop watch? Do I have good running shoes?	Do I have my equipment?	How do I feel about running?	Do I like my equipment? Do I like my route?
DURING:	**DURING:**	**DURING:**	**DURING:**
Does what I read about warm-up exercises and cool-down stretches make sense?	Am I performing all of the stretching exercises that I need to?	Is my motivation still strong?	How hard am I breathing? What is my heart rate?
AFTER:	**AFTER:**	**AFTER:**	**AFTER:**
Do I know what to do?	Did I cover the distance? What was my time?	Do I feel more relaxed? Is it getting easier?	What was my time? Do I feel healthier now?

Exercise

1. A 28-year-old expectant mother states her goal:

   "I want to eat healthier as indicated by the number of calories that I eat from each of the four basic food groups."

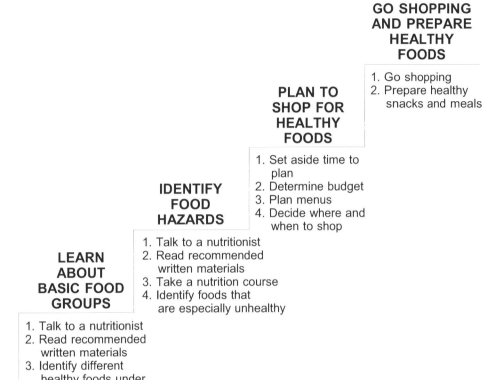

GO SHOPPING AND PREPARE HEALTHY FOODS
1. Go shopping
2. Prepare healthy snacks and meals

PLAN TO SHOP FOR HEALTHY FOODS
1. Set aside time to plan
2. Determine budget
3. Plan menus
4. Decide where and when to shop

IDENTIFY FOOD HAZARDS
1. Talk to a nutritionist
2. Read recommended written materials
3. Take a nutrition course
4. Identify foods that are especially unhealthy

LEARN ABOUT BASIC FOOD GROUPS
1. Talk to a nutritionist
2. Read recommended written materials
3. Identify different healthy foods under each food group

BEFORE:	BEFORE:	BEFORE:	BEFORE:
DURING:	DURING:	DURING:	DURING:
AFTER:	AFTER:	AFTER:	AFTER:

Exercise (continued)

2. A 20-year-old son states his goal:

    "I want to develop a better relationship with my father as indicated by the number of conversations I initiate with him."

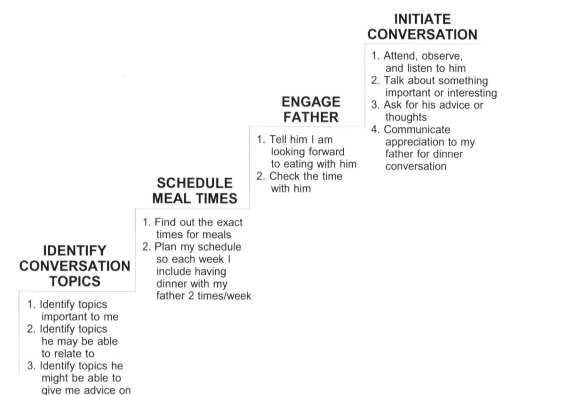

IDENTIFY CONVERSATION TOPICS

1. Identify topics important to me
2. Identify topics he may be able to relate to
3. Identify topics he might be able to give me advice on

SCHEDULE MEAL TIMES

1. Find out the exact times for meals
2. Plan my schedule so each week I include having dinner with my father 2 times/week

ENGAGE FATHER

1. Tell him I am looking forward to eating with him
2. Check the time with him

INITIATE CONVERSATION

1. Attend, observe, and listen to him
2. Talk about something important or interesting
3. Ask for his advice or thoughts
4. Communicate appreciation to my father for dinner conversation

BEFORE:	BEFORE:	BEFORE:	BEFORE:
DURING:	DURING:	DURING:	DURING:
AFTER:	AFTER:	AFTER:	AFTER:

III Summary

❻ Recycling the Helping Process

Overview

You have now learned and practiced a complete cycle of helping skills. You can use these skills with yourself and others to solve problems and achieve goals in living, learning, and working environments.

Exercise 57: Helping Yourself

Introduction

You have learned to help others to explore, understand, and act constructively. On the following pages, you will be using your responding, personalizing, and initiating skills to help yourself explore, understand, and act to solve a problem or take advantage of an opportunity.

Instructions

Follow the directions to complete each step.

Exercise

1. Briefly describe a current situation or experience in your life that you would like to transform into constructive action.

   _____

   _____

   _____

   _____

   _____

2. Write a series of six interchangeable responses to yourself. Be sure to give yourself time to continue to explore your current situation between each response.

   a. *1st* response to meaning: _____

   _____

   _____

   b. *2nd* response to meaning: _____

   _____

   _____

Exercise (continued)

    c. *3rd* response to meaning: _____

_____

_____

_____

    d. *4th* response to meaning: _____

_____

_____

_____

    e. *5th* response to meaning: _____

_____

_____

_____

    f. *6th* response to meaning: _____

_____

_____

_____

3. Personalize your experience. Be sure to take time to understand your role in your situation, its implications, and your current assumptions or beliefs about yourself and this situation before proceeding to develop the next personalized responses to yourself.

    a. **Response to personalized meaning:** _____

_____

_____

_____

    b. **Response to personalized meaning:** _____

_____

_____

_____

Exercise (continued)

c. **Response to personalized problem:** _____

_____

_____

_____

d. **Response to personalized goal:** _____

_____

_____

_____

4. Initiate to help yourself act on your personalized experience.

   Your operationalized goal: _____

   _____

   _____

   _____

   _____

   _____

5. Brainstorm steps to accomplish your operationalized goal.

   _____

   _____

   _____

   _____

   _____

   _____

   _____

   _____

   _____

   _____

Exercise (continued)

6. List steps and sub-steps to your goal:

START:

_____ _____ _____ _____ _____

FINISH:

_____ _____ _____ _____ _____

7. Initiate a schedule for yourself. Enter start and finish dates. Assume that you will begin your program today.

8. List reinforcements for yourself.

    a. **Positive Reinforcement(s):** _____

    _____

    b. **Negative Reinforcement(s):** _____

    _____

Exercise 58: Video or Audio Exercise 1

Introduction

The real challenge of helping occurs in the actual helping process. During a counseling session, the helping process is revisited and recycled. Effective helpers facilitate extensive exploration, accurate understanding, and effective acting by the helpee.

Instructions

If you have access to a video recording of any helping session, you can use the questions in this exercise to assist you in analyzing the processes that the helper in the video uses. (An audio recording may be used in the place of a video recording as only Question #1 requires *seeing* the helpee.)

Before viewing the video recording of a helping session, read the following questions and directions. Then, watch the video and answer the exercise questions.

Exercise

1. Begin by viewing the video recording and focusing your observation skills. After a few minutes, stop the video and record your observations and inferences about the helpee on the following chart.

Appearance	Behavior	Inference
Posture: Facial Expressions: Grooming: Body Build: Sex: ☐ Male ☐ Female Age: _____ Race:	Body Movements:	Energy Level: ☐ High ☐ Medium ☐ Low Feelings: ☐ Up ☐ Mixed ☐ Down

Exercise (continued)

2. As you watch the video, make a list of the feelings that the helpee is experiencing. You will see that as the helpee moves through exploration, understanding, and action, his/her feelings change. Also note if/when the helper communicates that he/she is in tune with these changing feelings by responding accurately to these feelings.

_____	_____
_____	_____
_____	_____
_____	_____
_____	_____
_____	_____
_____	_____
_____	_____
_____	_____
_____	_____

3. Watch and listen to the entire helping session. Does the helper use the skills of *attending, responding, personalizing,* and *initiating* to facilitate the helpee's movement through *exploration, understanding,* and *action*?

Imagine that the helpee is seated before you. Respond interchangeably (feeling and content) to the helpee early in the counseling session. Use the initial feeling words you listed as a basis for your responses.

3a. You feel _____ because _____

_____

3b. You feel _____ because _____

_____

3c. You feel _____ because _____

_____

4. Now personalize the meaning of the helpee's experience for the helpee.

You feel _____ because _____

_____

Exercise (continued)

5. Write a personalized response to communicate the helpee's problem.

   You feel _____ because you cannot _____

   _____

6. Communicate how the helpee feels about his/her deficit.

   You feel _____

7. What is the helpee's goal? Communicate the personalized goal.

   You feel _____ because you cannot _____

   _____

   and you want to _____

   _____

8. How does the helpee feel about the asset she/he wishes to have (the goal)?

   You feel _____

9. Next, operationalize the goal for the helpee. Do this by describing a "first step" in operational terms.

   Who or **What** is involved? _____

   What will be done? _____

   How and **Why** will it be done? _____

   When and **Where** will it be done? _____

   How Well will it be done? _____

10. Use this space to brainstorm some further steps that the helpee might take to reach her/his goal.

Exercise 59: Video or Audio Exercise 2

Introduction

Here is a second opportunity to practice your helping skills using a video or audio recording of an actual helping session.

Instructions

If you have access to a video recording of any helping session, you can use the questions in this exercise to assist you in analyzing the processes that the helper in the video uses. (An audio recording may be used in the place of a video recording as only Question #1 requires *seeing* the helpee.)

Before viewing the video recording of a helping session, read the following questions and directions. Then, watch the video and answer the exercise questions.

Exercise

1. Begin by viewing the video recording and focusing your observation skills. After a few minutes, stop the video and record your observations and inferences about the helpee on the following chart.

Appearance	Behavior	Inference
Posture:	Body Movements:	Energy Level:
		☐ High ☐ Medium ☐ Low
Facial Expressions:		
		Feelings:
		☐ Up ☐ Mixed ☐ Down
Grooming:		
Body Build:		
Sex: ☐ Male ☐ Female		
Age: _____		
Race:		

Exercise (continued)

2. As you watch the video, make a list of the feelings that the helpee is experiencing. You will see that as the helpee moves through exploration, understanding, and action, his/her feelings change. Also note if/when the helper communicates that he/she is in tune with these changing feelings by responding accurately to these feelings.

    _____   _____

    _____   _____

    _____   _____

    _____   _____

    _____   _____

    _____   _____

    _____   _____

    _____   _____

    _____   _____

    _____   _____

3. Watch and listen to the entire helping session. Does the helper use the skills of *attending, responding, personalizing,* and *initiating* to facilitate the helpee's movement through *exploration, understanding,* and *action*?

    Imagine that the helpee is seated before you. Respond interchangeably (feeling and content) to the helpee early in the counseling session. Use the initial feeling words you listed as a basis for your responses.

    3a. You feel _____ because _____

    _____

    3b. You feel _____ because _____

    _____

    3c. You feel _____ because _____

    _____

4. Now personalize the meaning of the helpee's experience for the helpee.

    You feel _____ because _____

    _____

Exercise (continued)

5. Write a personalized response to communicate the helpee's problem.

   You feel _____ because you cannot _____

   _____

6. Communicate how the helpee feels about his/her deficit.

   You feel _____

7. What is the helpee's goal? Communicate the personalized goal.

   You feel _____ because you cannot _____

   _____

   and you want to _____

   _____

8. How does the helpee feel about the asset she/he wishes to have (the goal)?

   You feel _____

9. Next, operationalize the goal for the helpee. Do this by describing a "first step" in operational terms.

   Who or **What** is involved? _____

   What will be done? _____

   How and **Why** will it be done? _____

   When and **Where** will it be done? _____

   How Well will it be done? _____

10. Use this space to brainstorm some further steps that the helpee might take to reach her/his goal.

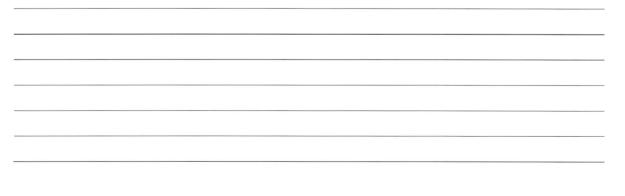

Post-Test

Overview

You have now practiced the basic skills of helping. At this point, you should review where you are in relation to these skills, both to see how far you have come and to begin to set new goals for yourself.

This two-page Post-Test will give you an opportunity to measure your ability to both *communicate* and *discriminate* helpful responses. (Once you have completed both the communication and discrimination post-test pages you may ask an expert (your teacher or trainer) to rate your communication post-test or you may refer to pages 175 or 176 of this workbook to help you rate your response yourself. You may turn to pages 173 of this workbook for answers to the discrimination post-test and to page 174 to record your ratings and calculate your discrimination score.

Part A. Post-Test: Communicating Helping Skills

Instructions

Imagine that you have been interacting with the following helpee for about 20 minutes. The helpee, a young executive in a retail business, says to you:

> *"I don't know what's going on. I get good performance reviews, but I don't seem to be able to get promoted to the next level. I was reviewed six months ago and I'm still waiting to move up. They say I'm doing excellent work, but one senior executive says I'm too aggressive and another says I'm not aggressive enough. I can't please everybody, yet it looks like I have to."*

Write down what you would say to this helpee. Write the exact words you would use if you were speaking to the helpee.

_____

_____

_____

_____

_____

_____

_____

Part B. Post-Test: Discriminating Helping Skills

Introduction

Throughout this workbook, you have learned to discriminate and communicate accurate and effective responses. This post-test will help to review the accuracy of your discriminations.

Instructions

Imagine that a young executive in a retail business has been talking to a helper for about 20 minutes. This is an excerpt of what the executive has been saying:

> *"I don't know what's going on. I get good performance reviews, but I don't seem to be able to get promoted to the next level. I was reviewed six months ago and I'm still waiting to move up. They say I'm doing excellent work, but one senior executive says I'm too aggressive and another says I'm not aggressive enough. I can't please everybody, yet it looks like I have to."*

Following are several alternative responses that might have been made by someone trying to help this person. Next to each response, write a number to indicate your rating of the effectiveness of that response. Use the following scale:

1.0 = Very Ineffective
2.0 = Ineffective
3.0 = Minimally Effective
4.0 = Very Effective
5.0 = Extremely Effective

Rating	Response
	a. You don't know what to make of the situation, how to please both parties so you can get promoted.
	b. You feel frustrated because you can't reach the level you're capable of and you want to learn what to do to move up.
	c. The business world is like that sometimes. They'll keep you there as long as they can if you're doing a good job. Only personalities get promoted!
	d. You feel stuck because you're not sure what you have to do to prove you're capable of handling the next level and you want to get the promotion. You might begin by discussing with your bosses what *behaviors* they see as aggressive or nonaggressive, then working out a compromise with them.
	e. You're confused because your bosses give you contradictory messages.

Post-Test Discrimination Ratings

Check your post-test discrimination ratings against the expert ratings.

Response	Rating	Reason
a.	2.0	An accurate response to content expressed by the helpee but the response does not include acknowledgement of the helpee's feeling(s).
b.	4.0	Response communicates the helpee's "internalized" experience and feelings, responsibility for his or her role in a problem or situation, and identifies a personal goal or solution.
c.	1.0	Response communicates non-attentiveness as both content and feeling are either absent or inaccurate.
d.	5.0	Response adds operational information about the goal and adds specific behavioral action steps for solving the problem and reaching the goal.
e.	3.0	Response to the helpee's feelings and "external reasons," (identified by the helpee as being beyond the helpee's control), for the situation and for the helpee's feelings.

A 5.0 is the highest rated response and a 1.0 is the lowest.

Post-Test Discrimination Scoresheet

To calculate your discrimination score, use the chart below and follow these steps:

1. Fill in your ratings for each of the five responses. These ratings indicate your ratings of the effectiveness of the five responses.

2. Without regard to whether the difference is positive or negative, write the difference between your ratings and the expert ratings. This will result in five "difference" scores, one for each response.

3. Add up the "difference" scores.

4. Divide the total of the "difference" scores by 5. The result is your discrimination score.

Response	My Rating		Expert Rating		Difference
a	_____	–	2.0	=	_____
b	_____	–	4.0	=	_____
c	_____	–	1.0	=	_____
d	_____	–	5.0	=	_____
e	_____	–	3.0	=	_____
			TOTAL	=	_____
		My Discrimination Score **(TOTAL ÷ 5)**		=	_____

A discrimination score of 0.0 is the highest rated.

Helper Communication Scales

Rating Helper Communications with 5-Point Scale

You may use the following 5-point scale to help you rate your own Communication Pre-Test and Post-Test. After your training experiences with *The Art of Helping,* you will find yourself able to skillfully measure any helper response against this 5-point scale.

LEVELS OF HELPING	
5.0 Initiating steps	Response adds operational information about the goal and adds specific behavioral action steps for solving the problem and reaching the goal.
4.0 Personalizing problem, goal, and feeling	Response communicates the helpee's "internalized" experience and feelings; responsibility for his or her role in a problem or situation, and identifies a personal goal or solution.
3.0 Responding to meaning	Response to the helpee's feelings and "external reasons" (identified by the helpee as being beyond the helpee's control), for the situation and for the helpee's feelings.
2.0 Responding to content	An accurate response to content expressed by the helpee but the response does not include acknowledgement of the helpee's feeling(s).
1.0 Non-attending	Response communicates non-attentiveness as both content and feeling are either absent or inaccurate.

Carkhuff's 5-point "Levels of Helping Scale" is a useful method for rating the effectiveness of helper responses in the service of helpee personal growth and problem-solving. (For an expanded 9-point scale, see the next page.)

Rating Helper Communications with 9-Point Scale

For a more detailed measurement, you may use the following expanded 9-point scale to help you rate your own Communication Pre-Test and Post-Test. After your training experiences with *The Art of Helping*, you will find yourself able to skillfully measure any helper response against this 9-point scale.

LEVELS OF HELPING	
5.0 Initiating steps	Response adds specific behavioral, action steps for solving problems and reaching goals.
4.5 Defining goals	Response adds operational information about the goal.
4.0 Personalizing problem, goal, and feeling	Response communicates the helpee's "internalized" experience and feelings; responsibility for his or her role in a problem or situation, and identifies a personal goal or solution.
3.5 Personalizing meaning	Response personalizes or internalizes meaning for the helpee's experience.
3.0 Responding to meaning	Response to the helpee's feelings and "external reasons" (identified by the helpee as being beyond the helpee's control), for the situation and for the helpee's feelings.
2.5 Responding to feeling	An accurate response to the helpee's feelings.
2.0 Responding to content	An accurate response to content expressed by the helpee.
1.5 Attending	Response does not respond accurately to the content that the helpee is expressing but may communicate some indirectly-related information or ask a relevant question.
1.0 Non-attending	Response communicates non-attentiveness as both content and feeling are either absent or inaccurate.

In the hands of a skilled rater, Carkhuff's well-researched 9-point "Levels of Helping Scale" is a useful method for rating the effectiveness of helper responses in the service of helpee personal growth and problem solving.

Pre-Test Ratings and Scoresheet

Pre-Test Discrimination Ratings

To check your pre-test discrimination ratings (from page 5) against expert ratings, here is a simple explanation. You will understand these ratings more fully after you have completed reading *The Art of Helping* text and completed the exercises in this workbook.

Response	Rating	Reason
a.	3.0	It communicates an accurate understanding of where the helpee is in terms of content and feelings expressed.
b.	1.0	It is not related to what the helpee said.
c.	5.0	It communicates an accurate understanding of where the helpee is, where she wants to be, and gives direction as to how she can get there. This response provides both understanding and direction.
d.	2.0	It is directly related to the content of the helpee's expression, but does not respond to feelings.
e.	4.0	It is an accurate response to both where the helpee is and where she wants to be.

A 5.0 is the highest rated response and a 1.0 is the lowest. Return to page 6, *Getting Ready for Training* and Exercise 1.

Pre-Test Discrimination Scoresheet

To calculate your discrimination score, use the chart below and follow these steps:

1. Fill in your ratings for each of the five responses. These ratings indicate your ratings of the effectiveness of the five responses.

2. Without regard to whether the difference is positive or negative, write the difference between your ratings and the expert ratings. This will result in five "difference" scores, one for each response.

3. Add up the "difference" scores.

4. Divide the total of the "difference" scores by 5. The result is your discrimination score.

Response	My Rating		Expert Rating		Difference
a	_____	−	*3.0*	=	_____
b	_____	−	*1.0*	=	_____
c	_____	−	*5.0*	=	_____
d	_____	−	*2.0*	=	_____
e	_____	−	*4.0*	=	_____
			TOTAL	=	_____
		My Discrimination Score **(TOTAL ÷ 5)**		=	_____

A discrimination score of 0.0 is the highest rated. Return to page 6, *Getting Ready for Training* and Exercise 1.

Answers

Answers to Selected Exercises

Exercise 8: Discriminating Self-Preparation Skills

1. Review Information: None—did not do it
   Review Goal: None—did not do it
   Relax (Eliminate Internal Distractions): Not Relaxed; Distracted—thinking about all that had gone wrong that day

2. Review Information: Looked at test scores and attendance
   Review Goal: No specific goal to review but knew that something drastic had to change or Mark would be receiving a failing grade
   Relax (Eliminate Internal Distractions): Closed eyes; let mind clear

3. Review Information: Reviewed Isabel's problematic behavior over the past months
   Review Goal: To tell her what he had noticed and to listen
   Relax (Eliminate Internal Distractions): Mental image of a trout stream

Exercise 11: Discriminating Data from Inferences

1. Inference		11. Inference	
2. Inference		12. Data	
3. Data		13. Data	
4. Inference		14. Data	
5. Data		15. Inference	
6. Data		16. Inference	
7. Inference		17. Inference	
8. Inference		18. Inference	
9. Data		19. Data	
10. Inference		20. Inference	

Exercise 12: Drawing Inferences from Observations

1. a, c, e	4. f	7. b, f
2. b, d, f	5. a, c	8. b
3. a, c	6. a, e	9. b, d, f
		10. b, f

Exercise 16: Discriminating Specific Responses

1.	Vague	4.	Specific
2.	Specific	5.	Vague
3.	Specific	6.	Vague

Exercise 17: Discriminating Paraphrasing vs. Parroting

1. a. Parrot
   b. Paraphrase
   c. Paraphrase

2. a. Paraphrase
   b. Parrot
   c. Paraphrase

Exercise 18: Discriminating Brief Responses

1. Brief and Specific
2. Brief and Specific
3. Too long
4. Too long
5. Brief and Specific

Exercise 19: Discriminating Good Content Responses

1. Poor; parrots
2. Poor; too vague
3. Good; specific, brief, and nonjudgmental
4. Poor; too long
5. Good; specific, brief, and nonjudgmental

Exercise 21: Discriminating Accurate Feeling Responses

1. a. + Accurate category and intensity
   b. − Inaccurate category (not angry but sad)
   c. + Accurate category and intensity

2. a. + Accurate category and intensity
   b. − Inaccurate category (not angry but sad)
   c. + Accurate category and intensity

3. a. + Accurate category and intensity
   b. − Inaccurate category (not angry but sad)
   c. + Accurate category (sad) but inaccurate intensity

Exercise 22: Choosing Accurate Feeling Words

1. a, c, d, i
2. b, d, e, h, i
3. a, e, f, h
4. a, c, e, g, i
5. a, c, e, g

Exercise 28: Discriminating Interchangeable Responses

1. a. Content not interchangeable; judgmental
   b. Good interchangeable response
   c. Wrong feeling word category
   d. Content is vague
   e. Wrong feeling word

2. a. No feeling word
   b. Content is vague
   c. Parrots the response
   d. Response is too long
   e. Good interchangeable response

Exercise 32: Discriminating Personalized Meaning Responses

1. IR
2. PM (Experience)
3. PM (Implications)
4. PM (Assumptions)

Exercise 34: Discriminating Personalized Problem Responses

1. a. PP
   b. IR
   c. PM

2. a. IR
   b. PM
   c. PP

3. a. PM
   b. IR
   c. PP

4. a. PP
   b. IR
   c. PM

Exercise 36: Discriminating Personalized Goal Behavior

1. a. New behavior
   b. Flip-side
   c. New behavior

2. a. Flip-side
   b. Flip-side
   c. New behavior

3. a. New behavior
   b. Flip-side
   c. New behavior

4. a. Flip-side
   b. New behavior
   c. Flip-side

Exercise 37: Discriminating Personalized Goals

1. a. IR
   b. IR
   c. PM
   d. PP
   e. PG

2. a. PM
   b. PM
   c. PP
   d. IR
   e. PG

3. a. PP
   b. PG
   c. PM
   d. PP
   e. IR

4. a. IR
   b. PM
   c. PP
   d. PG
   e. PP

Exercise 45: Making Sure the Steps to a Goal are Behaviors

1. Yes
2. Yes
3. No
4. No
5. No
6. Yes
7. Yes
8. Yes
9. Yes
10. No
11. No
12. Yes
13. No
14. Yes
15. No
16. No
17. No
18. Yes
19. No
20. No
21. Yes
22. No
23. Yes
24. No
25. Yes

Exercise 49: Discriminating Types of Reinforcements

1. a. Positive
   b. Negative
   c. Negative
   d. Positive

2. a. Negative
   b. Negative
   c. Positive
   d. Negative

3. a. Positive
   b. Positive
   c. Positive
   d. Negative

4. a. Negative
   b. Positive
   c. Positive
   d. Positive

5. a. Positive
   b. Negative
   c. Positive
   d. Positive

Made in the USA
Middletown, DE
31 July 2021